Daily Ma

# MONEY M
# SAVERS' GUIDE

## 1994–95

Daily Mail

# MONEY MAIL SAVERS' GUIDE

---

## 1994–95

---

First published in Great Britain in 1994 by Orion
An imprint of the Orion Publishing Group Ltd
Orion House, 5 Upper St Martin's Lane, London WC2H 9EA

A CIP catalogue record for this book is available from the British Library

ISBN 1-85592-820-5

Typeset by Selwood Systems, Midsomer Norton
Printed and bound in Great Britain by Butler & Tanner Ltd, Frome and London

# Contents

CHAPTER 1

# Why Save?

Nearly everyone saves at some point in his or her life if only for fairly obvious reasons, such as a deposit for a house, paying for a daughter's wedding or a new car.

Other people, even if they have no particular objective in mind, have a more or less continuous savings programme setting money aside on either a regular or more intermittent basis.

The Victorians identified it as the virtue thrift and although the nineteenth century connotations no longer apply – we don't need the protection of savings to avoid, at all costs, the fate of the workhouse – saving is still a good habit to acquire.

In the broadest possible terms, the money will always come in handy and, more importantly, it is a failsafe – should an emergency or personal disaster occur. Saving cannot prevent either happening, but it can alleviate some of the worst side effects.

But a vague appreciation that savings are "a good thing" is not really enough. To make the most of the very many different forms of savings and investment that are available, you do some preliminary fact-finding – about you.

For example, do you know exactly what your income is, let alone your after tax income? Do you know how much income you can expect in retirement? Are you panic-stricken at the thought of investment losing value? Do you even know what you want from your savings? Many people, it must be admitted, are a little woolly about the financial facts of life.

To help you decide (a) what you need from your savings and (b) the strategy to help you obtain it, answer the following basic questions.

## Can I afford to save?

If the answer to this question and the next four questions is "No", then you have problems. Some, such as long term unemployment where savings can almost be a positive disadvantage, may be intractable. (Income Support is only available in full for those with savings of £3,000 or less, with scaled down benefits for those with savings up to £8,000. For housing benefit and council tax benefit the ceiling is £16,000.) Others may be just a matter of making life-style adjustments.

Use the family budget planner on page **3** to work out just exactly where your disposable income goes. There are some interesting cost comparisons per month on page **4**. Each individual and family must decide their own priorities, but it is important that you can answer "yes" to the next four questions.

## Have I "rainy day" or emergency savings?

Advance notice is not given for most emergencies: the car clutch goes; the cistern bursts or a close member of your family working abroad becomes seriously ill. Can you afford the costs involved?

Before you begin any fancy footwork with exciting new investments such as new share issues, or even opt for higher interest on savings locked away for a longer time, make sure you have sufficient savings which are *immediately* available (or at the most can be withdrawn within two days).

The amount you need to save will vary from individual to individual, family to family. It should be £100–£300 at the very least and £500 is not too much for a single person. Married couples should think in terms of £1,000–£2,000 minimum. See Chapter Seven for more detailed analysis of suitable rainy day savings.

## Will my family be financially protected should I die or be permanently unable to work?

Mortgage payments, HP commitments, food costs, electricity bills and school fees (to mention but a few of the family's outgoings) won't stop if you die.

Life assurance (see pages **75–91**) is the principal means of making sure that your family or other dependants, such as elderly parents, will have financial security in the event of your death.

The cheapest form of life assurance, a good value-for-money buy, is *term assurance* – however, it is not included here because it has no investment content. It pays out only in the event of the policyholder's death. The cost is around £19.00 a month for a 30-year-old man wanting £100,000 of cover for 20 years. Nor are the policies which cover you against sickness or accident included here.

- How much life insurance cover? As a very rough guide, think in terms of up to five times earnings. But don't forget that if you have
- *An endowment mortgage* – this should repay the house loan
- Or belong to a *company pension scheme* – you might have death cover up to four times salary built into the scheme. Should you leave the pension scheme that benefit will disappear, unless you join a similar scheme.

## Am I satisfied with my present living accommodation?

If you are renting a flat or house, or sharing with your parents, the answer will probably be "No". In which case you need to start saving, hard, for your own home, and to get your feet on the housing ladder. It is sometimes possible to obtain 100 per cent home loans, but it is still wise to save (see Chapter Seven).

- It will get you in the habit of setting aside a large sum each month; otherwise you might find these monthly mortgage payments a bit of a shock.
- If you have a deposit, you might not have to pay the one-off premium of a mortgage guarantee insurance policy which lenders require on loans above 70–85 per cent of the house price.
- Legal fees, moving expenses and furnishings will eat into any savings, even if you don't need or wish for a deposit.

## Am I saving enough for my retirement?

To a certain extent *all* of your savings can be described, ultimately, as being for your retirement.

But there will be many other calls and temptations on your funds between now and then, so it is important to have some savings and investments which are not only specifically earmarked for retirement, but cannot be taken except as a pension.

Chapter Seven looks at this subject in more detail; and at the ways of improving your retirement income if you feel that, hitherto, you have been a little lax in respect of this essential saving.

## OUTGOINGS PER MONTH
### Unavoidable expenditure

FOOD . . . . . . . £______

HOUSING

Mortgage/rent . . . . . £______

Ground rent . . . . . . £______

Water rates . . . . . . £______

Council tax . . . . . . £______

HEATING

Electricity . . . . . . £______

Gas . . . . . . . £______

Other fuel etc. . . . . . £______

INSURANCE

Contents . . . . . . £______

Building . . . . . . . £______

Life assurance. . . . . . £______

Motor . . . . . . . £______

Mortgage protection . . . £______

Other . . . . . . . £______

TRAVEL

Season ticket . . . . . . £______

Car tax . . . . . . . £______

Maintenance payments . . . £______

Child care . . . . . . £______

Other . . . . . . . £______

TOTAL £______

## SAVINGS

PAY council tax and water rates by instalments. PAY bills together through Giro to save postage and bank charges. PAY car tax for the full year. COMBINED house and buildings insurance can be cheaper. BUY the longest season ticket possible. INSULATE the house for substantial saving on energy bills. TURNING down the thermostat 4°F can save 10 per cent on heating bills. CHECK out school shops for second-hand school clothes. BUY own brand food.

## TAX TIPS

KEEP mortgage to £30,000 for maximum tax relief. BE wary of switching to another lender if your existing mortgage covers home improvements made before 6 April 1988. You could lose tax relief on this part of the new loan. CHECK your PAYE notice of coding (sent in January and February) to make sure all the allowances to which you are entitled are there. HIGHER rate taxpayers and people with income from other sources should check their Schedule E Notice of Assessment which explains how the Revenue has worked out your tax bill. If you disagree, appeal within 30 days.

## DON'TS

DON'T buy gas, electricity or telephone stamps, but put money into a building society. DON'T pay for gas or electricity through a slot meter. DON'T heat unused rooms. DON'T over-insure. DON'T cash in a life insurance policy early; surrender values are poor. DON'T cash in any life insurance bought before March 1984; you will lose valuable tax relief. NEVER pay in advance if you can pay in arrears.

| | *Cost per month* |
|---|---|
| Twenty filter-tip cigarettes a day at £2.52 a pack | £75.60 |
| Shampoo and set at £9 a week | £36.00 |
| Two pints of beer a day at £1.60 a pint | £89.60 |
| Cat food at £2.80 a week | £11.20 |
| Two weekly magazines at 50p per week | £4.00 |
| Pocket money for 14–16-year-olds at £3.60 per week (TSB's pocket money survey) | £14.40 |
| Mortgage protection plan for 25 years for a 35-year-old man per £50,000 house loan | £7.75 |
| Unit trust monthly savings plan | £25.00 |
| Minimum holding in National Savings Certificates | £100 |
| Minimum monthly savings – Personal Equity Plan | £25–£30 |
| Bank and building society account can be opened for as little as | £1–£5 |

**OUTGOINGS PER MONTH**
**Other essentials**

| | |
|---|---|
| Petrol | |
| Other fares | £_____ |
| TV licence | £_____ |
| School fees/ clothes | £_____ |
| Pension contributions | £_____ |
| Telephone | £_____ |
| Garage repairs | £_____ |
| Medical/Dentist | £_____ |
| LOANS | |
| HP | £_____ |
| Personal loan | £_____ |
| Overdraft | £_____ |
| TOTAL | £_____ |

# Additional checks

## Life assurance

If you really do have life policies which are surplus to requirements and need to cash them in (rather than making them "paid up"), you will get more money from selling the policies than surrendering them. There is a brisk market in second-hand policies. The Association of Policy Market Makers (0621–851133) will provide a list of companies which deal in second-hand policies.

## Telephone charges: BT

*Daytime rate* (from 9 March 1994): Mon–Fri 8am–6pm
*Cheap rate:* Mon–Fri 6pm to 8am
Sat & Sun all day

*Each unit is 4.2p (excluding VAT)*
*Local calls* – within exchange
Daytime: 80 seconds;
cheap: 220 seconds.
*Trunk calls* (A Rate – up to 56.4 kilometres)
Daytime: 36.15 seconds;
cheap: 80.8 seconds.
*Trunk calls* (B Rate – over 56.4 kilometres)
Daytime: 32 seconds; cheap: 50.35 seconds.

**SAVINGS**

TELEPHONE during cheap rate periods. PAY regular bills by standing order, better still direct debit, to save postage. SEARCH out interest-free credit offers. An OVERDRAFT is cheaper than a personal loan if you can get one. DRIVE carefully to conserve petrol. CONVERT your car to unleaded petrol, it's cheaper. PAY school fees in advance: can be 40 per cent cheaper. ALWAYS check for hidden charges in any credit deal. CHECK bank statements thoroughly. LIMIT directory enquiry calls (now 43.5p a time) or use a payphone which still allows free directory enquiries. CONVERT your current account to one which pays interest.

### TAX TIPS

TAKE out as large a pension as you can afford. A pension-linked mortgage, with tax relief on the mortgage interest (up to £30,000 of loan) and pension contributions, is very tax efficient.

### DON'TS

DON'T borrow money to pay off debts. DON'T go into the red without consulting your bank manager; bank charges on unauthorised borrowings are high. BANK budget accounts cost a lot; organise your own system. DON'T spend money wrongly credited to your account; it has to go back. DON'T raise a loan on trading cheques; rates are astronomical.

### OUTGOINGS PER MONTH
#### Important costs

HOUSEHOLD

| | |
|---|---|
| Kitchen equipment | £_____ |
| Cleaning and toiletries | £_____ |
| Hairdressing | £_____ |
| Decorating | £_____ |
| Birthday, Xmas presents | £_____ |
| Holidays. | £_____ |
| Evening classes | £_____ |
| Pocket money. | £_____ |
| Garden tools | £_____ |
| Trade union fees | £_____ |
| Vet | £_____ |
| TV rental | £_____ |
| School trips | £_____ |
| Other | £_____ |
| TOTAL | £_____ |

## Overdraft interest

Your bank manager will almost invariably suggest a bank personal loan – which costs more than an overdraft. What is more, the interest rate is fixed for the duration of the loan, irrespective of what might happen to interest rates. Discuss your credit arrangements with him/her. Most managers will probably accede to your request for an overdraft. Then negotiate for the interest rate: overdraft rates range from 2½ per cent to 6 per cent over bank base rates. Most customers will be fobbed off with 5 per cent: persuade your bank manager to go lower.

One of the cheapest forms of overdraft credit is available to holders of "Gold" cards – the up-market charge or credit cards which have a built-in automatic overdraft facility up to £10,000, by negotiation.

### SAVINGS

BUY in bulk if there is room for storage. SEARCH out grants wherever these might be available; they are free gifts. CHECK your credit card terms: balance a flat initial fee with a lower interest rate (suitable if you use the credit regularly) against no fee and a higher interest rate. INSURE pets when they are young to cover later vet's bills. SOME subscriptions offer discount for paying by direct debit. USE customer discount cards where available.

## TAX TIPS

USE child's tax relief allowance wherever possible; have money gifts made direct to a child. CHILDREN can earn up to £3,445 a year before paying tax.

## DON'TS

DON'T rent household equipment, televisions, video recorders and compact disc players; it's cheaper to buy. This includes telephones, but make sure you buy one that has been approved for connection to British Telecom lines – it will carry a green circle.

## Pensions 1:

Many self-employed are wary about tying up the maximum possible into their private pension arrangements despite the attractive element of tax relief built into such schemes. Pension fund monies cannot be released (as a pension or permitted cash commutation) until stated retirement age.

## OUTGOINGS PER MONTH
### Flexible costs

| | |
|---|---|
| Clothes | £______ |
| Furnishing | £______ |
| Magazines and newspapers | £______ |
| Cosmetics | £______ |
| Postage and stationery | £______ |
| Garden | £______ |
| Laundry | £______ |
| Xmas entertainment | £______ |
| Credit cards | £______ |
| Savings | £______ |
| TOTAL | £______ |

However, it is always possible to activate the pension plan "loan back" arrangements should an urgent need for cash emerge in the meantime.

## Pensions 2:

Anyone not belonging to a company pension scheme can get tax relief up to 17.5 per cent of net relevant earnings (more once you are 36). If you haven't paid the maximum allowed in any of the previous six tax years, you can top up those contributions and obtain tax relief for those years.

## SAVINGS

LEARN a money-making skill at evening classes. SHOP at sale times. BE cheeky and ask for discount for cash wherever appropriate. DUAL pricing is now allowed; pay by cash if it is cheaper than using a credit card. PAY credit card bill in full every month to avoid interest charges; some cards now charge interest from the purchase date if the account is not cleared that month. AVOID store cards which usually have a higher interest rate than bank credit cards. PAY store cards, if you insist on using them, by direct debit if you can't repay in full, as the interest charge is often lower. This is the case with some credit cards too.

## TAX TIPS

HIGHER rate taxpayers should look for tax-free investments such as National Savings Certificates, Tessas and PEPs (see individual sections for details). NON-taxpayers should go for investments that pay interest gross and register to receive interest without deduction of tax (otherwise it will be paid and a time interval will occur before the tax can be reclaimed). A wife's investment income can now be offset against her personal tax allowance, so a non-working wife's savings should be in gross-paying investments to "use up" her personal allowance. Since April 1991 banks and building societies have been able to pay interest gross to non-taxpayers.

**DON'TS**

DON'T buy clothes that can't go in the washing machine; dry cleaning costs are high. DON'T use store cards when their interest charges are higher than others.

## Direct debits

Not only are some subscriptions cheaper if you pay by direct debit, but you might also save money if payments are debited from your account this way rather than by paying for the bills with more expensive-to-handle (from the bank's point of view) cheques, as some banks still charge more for cheque withdrawals. Of course, this charge only applies if your account is not in credit – free banking, although not universally available, with the majority of bank accounts applies when the account is in the black.

**OUTGOINGS PER MONTH**
**Desirable costs**

| | |
|---|---|
| Charity donations | £_____ |
| Eating out | £_____ |
| Cinema and theatre | £_____ |
| Alcohol and tobacco | £_____ |
| Hobbies/sport | £_____ |
| Toys | £_____ |
| Books | £_____ |
| Records/tapes | £_____ |
| Gambling | £_____ |
| Office collections | £_____ |
| TOTAL | £_____ |

**SAVINGS**

SOME theatres and cinemas sell half-price seats on Mondays. MATINEE performances are cheaper and less crowded. PENSIONER price concessions are often available. SET menus offer far better value than à la carte.

**TAX TIPS**

MAKE charitable donations under covenant or the gift aid scheme (for lump sums) for tax advantage. CONSIDER using a credit card which makes donations to named charities related to the amount cardholders spend. GAMBLING winnings are tax free.

**DON'TS**

DON'T sell any valuables to doorstep hawkers; get comparative valuations. DON'T spend needlessly on children.

## Company loans

Cheap or interest-free company loans, for example, to buy an expensive season ticket could result in a higher tax bill. The Inland Revenue counts it as a taxable benefit, assessing the value according to the "official rate of interest" applied to the loan.

Provided the loan does not exceed £5,000, no tax will be charged.

## Consolidation loans

It is tempting to take out a consolidation loan to take care of all existing debts, but many debts – such as gas, electricity and telephone bills – are renewed every few months. As a rule of thumb, the borrowing term should not exceed the life span of the asset you are buying. For example, cars are renewed every two to three years; holidays come round once a year; electricity and other service bills once a quarter. Tailor your borrowing accordingly so that you have repaid one loan before the next one is taken out.

## Interest-free credit

Although this is valuable, do make sure that the store or shop which is offering it is not charging a price at the upper end of the scale. With hi-fi and some "white" goods, the prices in discount stores might be sufficiently attractive to outweigh a temporary interest charge or loss of interest if you mobilise savings to buy them. Shopping around can be both tedious, time-consuming and only marginally beneficial: sometimes – and with these kind of goods in particular – it can be very worthwhile.

## Rented equipment

If you still prefer to rent your TV and similar equipment, keep an eye on the tariff and standard of equipment currently offered by the renter. You might be paying a rate, fixed some time ago, on equipment which is now let for a lower rental, or could "swap" your CD and video recorder, say, for a more comprehensive system for the same price.

CHAPTER 2

# From Safety First to High Risk

The difference between savings and investment is that the former is safer than investment which will always involve some element of risk. Understanding the risk spectrum from "safety first" to "high risk" is an important aspect of managing one's money well and deciding the most appropriate savings strategy (see Chapter Eight).

To help readers of *Money Mail Savers' Guide* we have devised a ratings guide which identifies the degree of investment risk that different kinds of savings and investment have.

## Money Mail Rating

**Safe *******
**Sound ****!**
**Opportunity **!!!**
**Aggressive *!!!!**
**Risky !!!!!**

It is an at-a-glance ratings symbol which gives readers a quick guide to the kind of investment they might be contemplating. The second half of this book, which goes through each investment one-by-one, uses this rating.

The qualities which determine an investment's risk are whether the capital value is fixed or varies; whether the rate of interest is fixed; the currency; whether the investment is narrowly or widely spread; and the market for those investments.

So the spectrum ranges from National Savings Certificates to unquoted foreign companies.

The various investment categories are:

- Fixed capital, fixed interest
- Fixed capital, variable interest
- Variable capital, fixed interest
- Variable capital, variable interest
- Variable capital, variable interest, variable currency
- Variable capital, no interest

## Fixed capital, fixed interest

This type of investment is the safest of all. The investor knows, at any time, exactly what he will obtain from his money.

In this category are:

**Bank, Deposit Taker and Offshore**

Term Accounts
Tax Exempt Special Savings Accounts

**Life Insurance**

Guaranteed Growth & Income Bonds – provided they are held to maturity
School Fees Educational Trust
Annuity

**Local Authority**
Loans
Corporation Stock } provided they are held
Yearling Bond } to maturity
**National Savings**
Capital Bonds
First Option Bond
Pensioners Guaranteed Income Bond
41st Issue National Savings Certificates
Yearly Plan
**Stock**
Government fixed interest – provided held to maturity
*Money Mail Rating* *****

## Fixed capital, variable interest

This form of investment is very safe, because the investor can always get his original capital back in full, even though the rate of interest it earns may vary.
In this category are:
**Bank and Deposit Takers**
Deposit Account
Children's Account
High Interest Cheque Account
High Interest Deposit Account
Monthly Savings Account
Notice Account
Tax Exempt Special Savings Account
**Building Society**
Cash Card Account
Cheque Book Account
Children's Account
Instant Access Account
Monthly Income
Monthly Savings Account
Notice Account
Offshore Share Account
Tax Exempt Special Savings Account
Term Share
**Life Insurance**
With-Profits Endowment – provided they are held to maturity
With-Profits Flexible Endowment – provided they are held to guaranteed surrender dates
**National Savings**
Income Bonds
Investment Account
Ordinary Account
Index-Linked Certificates
Premium Bonds
**Offshore**
High Interest Cheque Account
**Pensions**
Additional Voluntary Contributions
Transfer Plan
*Money Mail Rating* *****

## Variable capital, fixed interest

Such investment is moving out of the very safe category. Although the interest remains fixed, there can be wide fluctuations in capital values, leaving the investor hopefully better off, but maybe worse off. These investments are therefore not suitable for emergency funds. In this category are:
**Variable capital, fixed**
Government and Local Authority Stock – unless held to redemption
Company Loan and Debenture Stock – unless held to redemption
Preference Shares
*Money Mail Rating* ****! *to* **!!!

## Variable capital, variable interest

This covers a very wide range of share investments, with different degrees of risk which depend upon the size, track record and marketability of individual shares in different companies, and whether or not the investment is widely spread, to narrow the risk over the range of shares. But they are all risky investments in which an investor can see his capital dwindle, occasionally disappear, and his income suffer the same fate.
**Shares**
Companies listed on the Stock Exchange, including Personal Equity Plans.

*Money Mail Rating* ****! *to* *!!!!

Smaller and younger companies with shares quoted on the Stock Exchange's own Unlisted Securities Market.

*Money Mail Rating* **!!! *to* !!!!!

**Investment Trusts**

including Personal Equity Plans

**Unit Trusts**

including Personal Equity Plans

*Money Mail Rating* ****! *to* *!!!!

**Life Assurance**

Friendly Society Savings Plan

Investment Bonds

Unit-Linked Savings

*Money Mail Rating* ****! *to* *!!!!

## Variable capital, variable interest, variable currency

Currencies rise and fall in value against each other, and investments which have to get the currency right as well as the underlying investments have a very high risk factor. Investment managers admit that selecting the right currency and "hedging" (to minimise the risk) is one of their most difficult tasks.

**Offshore**

Currency Funds

Unit Trusts

*Money Mail Rating* **!!! *to* !!!!!

## Variable capital, no interest

Investments such as commodities, precious metals, antiques which may not be easily marketable

Gold

Offshore funds investing in alternative investments

*Money Mail Rating* *!!!! *to* !!!!!

CHAPTER 3

# Tax and Savings

If the most fundamental reasons for saving are *emergencies, family protection, house purchase* and *provision for old age*, the most significant feature underlying your savings and investment decisions after assessing the *risk factor* is *tax*, which affects the return you get on your investments.

Some forms of investment and savings are more suitable for higher rate taxpayers; others will be of more benefit to those who pay little or no tax.

Both income and capital gains are now taxed at the same rates: either 25 per cent or 40 per cent. Capital gains tax liabilities sit on top of income, and could push you into the 40 per cent bracket if your *total* taxable income plus taxable gains exceeds £23,700.

To make the most of the wide variety of savings discussed in greater detail later, it is sensible to get to grips with the tax system and how it affects you and your family.

## Income tax

Contrary to general myth we don't pay tax on all our income. Everyone, from the youngest baby in the country to the oldest pensioner, is entitled to some tax-free income (assuming, of course, that they have some income). In addition, some state benefits are tax free, some expenditure is given tax relief and the interest on certain forms of savings is tax free.

The principal tax-free *allowances* vary according to marital status and age, and whether you are a single-parent family (see tax table on page 14).

Certain outgoings are given tax relief up to a certain amount. These include:

- Mortgage interest relief at 20 per cent rate of tax only (dropping to 15 per cent from April 1995) on home loans up to £30,000.
- Pension scheme contributions of up to 15 per cent of your earnings if employed, or 17½ per cent if self-employed or not in a company pension scheme, rising with a personal pension plan to 20 per cent at age 36 and increasing to a maximum of 40 per cent at age 61 and over, qualify for tax relief at your top rate of tax. (From age 36 contributions are less generous for the old-style retirement annuities.) Members of company pension schemes who joined after 1 June 1989 will be restricted to tax relief on pension scheme contributions on earnings up to £76,800 only. The same limits apply to personal pension plans taken out since 6 April 1989.
- Maintenance and alimony payments made before 15 March 1988 are given tax relief; on agreements made from 15 March 1988 relief is given up to a limit equal to the difference between the single and married person's allowance.

- Covenanted payments to charities attract tax relief at basic and higher rate tax.
- Life assurance policies taken out before 13 March 1984 qualify for tax relief at 12½ per cent.
- Payroll deductions to charity up to a maximum donation of £75 a month qualify for tax relief.
- Individual gifts to charity over £250 are tax free. Gifts are paid net of basic rate tax; higher rate tax relief is claimed by the taxpayer.

Income and savings which are exempt from income tax are:

- National Savings Bank Ordinary Account – the first £70 of interest a year.
- National Savings Certificates (index-linked as well as conventional).
- National Savings Yearly Plan – the interest.
- Premium Bond prizes.
- Save As You Earn (SAYE) bonuses.
- Personal Equity Plan – dividends, whether they are reinvested or distributed.
- Tax Exempt Special Savings Account (Tessa) – tax free if held for five years; if income is withdrawn earlier it is paid net; the tax withheld is paid as a tax-free bonus after five years.
- Life assurance policies – the proceeds of qualifying policies (usually where regular payments are in force) paid out either at death or after 7½–10 years.
- Annuities – a proportion of the annuity income which varies with age.
- Football pools – the winnings; and other betting winnings (although you may have to pay betting tax).
- Maintenance payments – on agreements made from 15 March 1988.
- Redundancy payments – up to £30,000.

**Benefits which are not taxable and which should not be entered on your tax return include:**

Child benefit
Mobility allowance
One-parent benefit
Guardian's allowance and child's special allowance
Income support
Industrial disablement benefits
Severe disablement allowance
Christmas bonus paid with state pension or allowance
Child dependency additions
Family credit
Sickness benefit
Housing benefit
Attendance allowance
Social fund payments
Maternity allowance
Invalidity benefit
Widow's payment

**Pensions which are non-taxable and should not be entered on your tax return include:**

War widows' pension.
Certain pensions for wounds or disability caused or aggravated by military service or for other war injuries.
Pensions paid to victims of Nazi persecution by the German or Austrian governments should be entered, although special provisions apply.

**Grants which are non-taxable and should not be entered on your tax return include:**

Assisted places grant
Student grant

## Working out your tax bill

Basic rate is only levied on your *taxable income*: this is your income after deducting your allowances and permitted outgoings and ignoring, of course, tax-free income.

There is a reduced rate band of 20 per cent on the first £3,000 of income. Basic rate tax is currently 25 per cent on taxable income between £3,000 and £23,700; anything over that is taxed at 40 per cent.

There are 24.5 million taxpayers, of whom 1,700,000 pay higher rate tax.

Pensioners who are reliant on the state retirement pension only are unlikely to be taxpayers, but need to be very careful that modest savings which are taxed at source don't tip them into the basic rate tax bracket (see Chapter Five).

## Income Tax Rates

| Taxable Income | | Rate | Tax payable |
|---|---|---|---|
| | £ | % | £ |
| 1994–95 | 0– 3,000 | 20 | 600 |
| | 3,001–23,700 | 25 | 5,800 |
| | over 23,701 | 40 | |
| 1993–94 | 0– 2,500 | 20 | 500 |
| | 2,501–23,700 | 25 | 5,300 |
| | over 23,701 | 40 | |
| | | 1994–95 | 1993–94 |
| Additional rate (discretionary trusts) | | 10 | 10 |

## Income Tax allowances

| | 1994–95 | 1993–94 |
|---|---|---|
| | £ | £ |
| Personal | 3,445 | 3,445 |
| Married couple* | 1,720 | 1,720 |
| Additional personal and widow's bereavement | 1,720 | 1,720 |
| Personal (65–74) | 4,200 | 4,200 |
| Married couple (65–74)* | 2,665 | 2,465 |
| Personal (75 plus) | 4,370 | 4,370 |
| Married couple (75 plus)* | 2,705 | 2,505 |
| Blind person's** | 1,200 | 1,080 |
| Age allowance income limit† | 14,200 | 14,200 |

* This is in addition to the personal allowance which *each* spouse receives; in the first instance it is given to the husband (at lower 20 per cent rate only for 1994–95).

** Reduced by any tax-free disability benefit received.

† Once income exceeds £14,200 the age allowance is reduced by £1 for every £2 of income until it reaches the level of the normal allowances. The extra personal allowance runs out at £15,710 (age 65–74) or £16,050 (75 plus); for the partner claiming the married couple's allowance at £17,600 (65–74) or £17,680 (75 plus).

## Trust income

Using trusts for both convenience and tax planning has a long history. There are basically three kinds of trust: income in possession trusts, discretionary trusts, and accumulation and maintenance trusts.

Interest in possession trusts, which give the beneficiary the right to the trust income, are widely used for inheritance tax planning as the lifetime gift to the trust is a PET – that is a Potentially Exempt Transfer. Provided the settlor survives seven years after making the gift, it will pass beyond the inheritance tax net (see page **18**). The beneficiary pays income tax at his or her appropriate tax rate.

The beneficiary of a discretionary trust does not have the automatic right to income; as the name indicates, it is at the discretion of the trustees. This affects the tax treatment of the income. There is a special rate of tax for discretionary trusts which is basic rate tax (25 per cent) plus an additional rate (10 per cent), making a combined total of 35 per cent.

If the income is distributed to a child or other non-taxpayer, the 35 per cent tax paid can be reclaimed. With a child, use tax form R232 to reclaim the tax. However, if the parent has settled the gift, the child's trust income will be aggregated with his own.

Accumulation and maintenance trusts, used often to provide school fees, work in a similar way. It is quite possible that the income will not be distributed immediately, in which case the trustees will pay the 35 per cent tax on the trust fund's income. This can then be paid out later as capital without a further charge to tax.

The big difference between discretionary trusts and accumulation and maintenance trusts is in respect of inheritance tax. Gifts into the former are not PETs, but are subject to inheritance tax at the reduced lifetime rate of 20 per cent. Gifts into the latter trust, provided the settlor survives seven years, are exempt from inheritance tax.

Trusts are very useful for helping with estate and tax planning where substantial sums are involved. It costs £300–£500 to set up a trust.

## CHAPTER 4

# Capital Taxes

Income tax isn't the only tax you must consider; the capital taxes – capital gains tax and inheritance tax (formerly capital transfer tax) – can have some bearing on your investment decisions.

## Capital gains tax

If you make a profit when you sell an asset (or indeed give it away for more than its acquisition value) then you have made a capital gain. Conversely, you might have a capital loss on your hands if the asset has decreased in value before you sell or part with it.

In each tax year capital gains, less capital losses and any expenses incurred in buying and selling (such as legal fees or commission), are, if they exceed a certain level, subject to capital gains tax at either 25 per cent or 40 per cent. Your taxable gains are aggregated with your income to determine which rate you pay (see Chapter Three).

There are several comforting facts to remember about capital gains tax.

- Many types of assets are exempt from capital gains tax.
- Capital gains tax only applies to the *gains* you make, not the actual disposal price.
- The level at which the tax begins is sufficiently high – £5,800 in tax year 1994–95 – to keep many investors out of this tax net.
- Only gains accrued since 31 March 1982 will be taxable.
- The indexation of capital gains made since March 1982, which "increases" the purchase price of your asset in line with the rise in the retail price index, makes it even less likely that capital gains tax will apply.
- Capital losses can be offset against taxable gains, but can also, if not used in one tax year, be carried forward indefinitely to set against capital gains you might make in the future. However, losses on disposals made after 29 November 1994 cannot be increased in line with indexation.
- No capital gains tax is paid at death: whoever inherits your assets does so at the market value at your death.

## Principal assets exempt from capital gains tax

You will not have to pay capital gains tax on the disposal of the following assets:

**Your principal home** If you have more than one house you can select which is your main home provided the choice is made within three years of buying the second. You can subsequently change your mind, but can only back-date your choice by two years.

**Your car**

**Your "chattels"** – personal belongings such as furniture and jewellery sold for £6,000 or less; gallantry decorations you have earned, not bought, are totally exempt.

**National Savings** Certificates, Yearly Plan, Capital Bond, First Option Bond, Pensioners Guaranteed Income Bond, Save As You Earn (SAYE) and Premium Bond prizes.

**British Government stock** and company loan or debenture stock.

**Legal tender** (which still includes gold sovereigns, half sovereigns and the Britannia gold coins) and any foreign currency obtained for personal use abroad.

**Personal Equity Plan**

**Tax Exempt Special Savings Accounts**

**Business Expansion Scheme** shares held for qualifying five years.

**Enterprise Investment Scheme** shares held for qualifying five years.

**Tangible movable property** with a predictable life of no more than 50 years such as boats, caravans and animals.

**Life insurance policies** of which you are the original owner.

**Gifts** to charities or the nation.

## Indexation of capital gains

Inflation, as opposed to real growth in the value of any assets you subsequently sell, is taken into account by linking the purchase price with the change in the Retail Price Index since then.

This has the effect of "increasing" the purchase price and thereby reducing or even eliminating your capital gain altogether. In the latter case, it has actually created a capital loss. By the same token indexation can increase an existing loss.

On post 31 March 1982 gains, use the Retail Price Index for the appropriate month (see page **173**) to work out the index-linked value which is to be added to your original purchase price.

For example, take shares bought in August 1984 for £3,000 and sold for £6,000 in January 1987. The Retail Price Index rose by 10.8 per cent between August 1984 and December 1986. As 10.8 per cent of £3,000 is £324, that amount of index-linked value must be added to your original purchase price of £3,000, bringing it to £3,324 and thus reducing the capital gain to £2,676. Losses made on disposals after 29 November 1994 cannot be increased in line with indexation.

## Inheritance tax

Inheritance tax replaced capital transfer tax on 18 March 1986. It bears more resemblance to the old estate duty (which was itself replaced by capital transfer tax) in that only gifts at death (or near) are taxable.

Substantial exemptions from inheritance tax are allowed and in addition the first £150,000 of gifts or bequests is also exempt from the tax. The balance attracts tax at 40 per cent (other than lifetime gifts to discretionary trusts where the rate is 20 per cent).

However, substantial house price inflation means that many people who might hitherto have considered they had "little to leave" might find their estate liable to this tax.

All gifts made seven years before death are tax free. All non-exempt gifts made within three years of death are liable to inheritance tax and included in your estate. Gifts made between three and seven years are taxed on a sliding scale.

### Inheritance tax rates from 6 April 1992

| Portion of value £,000 | On death* Rate of tax |
|---|---|
| 0–150 | Nil |
| Over 150 | 40% |

### Inheritance tax rates from 6 April 1991

| Portion of value £,000 | On death* Rate of Tax |
|---|---|
| 0–140 | Nil |
| Over 140 | 40% |

* Also applies to any gift made within three years of death.

## Gifts exempt from inheritance tax

- Gifts between husband and wife.
- Gifts of £3,000 in each tax year; an unused portion can be brought forward one year.
- Wedding gifts: parents – £5,000 each; grandparents, great-grandparents and bride and groom to each other – £2,500; anyone else – £1,000.
- Any number of individual gifts not exceeding £250 (provided the recipient has not received gifts under the two previous headings).
- Money spent on your child's maintenance and education; reasonable provision for care of dependent relative.
- "Normal expenditure" gifts out of taxed income (*not* capital), the making of which does not affect your standard of living.
- Gifts to charities.
- Gifts to museums, art galleries and the National Trust including property of "outstanding national interest".

### Gifts made within seven years of death

| | % taxable |
|---|---|
| more than seven years before | 0 |
| more than six years before | 20 |
| more than five years before | 40 |
| more than four years before | 60 |
| more than three years before | 80 |
| less than three years before | 100 |

## Free tax leaflets from the Inland Revenue

| *Booklet no.* | *Title* |
|---|---|
| IR1 | Extra-statutory concessions |
| IR4 | Income tax and Pensioners |
| IR4A | Income Tax – Age Allowance |
| IR11 | Tax Treatment of Interest Paid |
| IR13 | Income Tax – Wife's Earnings Election |
| IR20 | Residents and Non-Residents – Liability to tax in the United Kingdom |
| IR22 | Income Tax – Personal Allowances |
| IR23 | Income Tax and Widows |
| IR24 | Class 4 National Insurance Contributions |
| IR28 | Starting in Business |
| IR33 | Income Tax and School Leavers |
| IR34 | Income Tax – Pay As You Earn |
| IR41 | Income Tax and the Unemployed |
| IR42 | Income Tax – Lay-offs and short time work |
| IR43 | Income Tax and Strikes |
| IR45 | Income Tax, Capital Gains Tax and Capital Transfer Tax – What happens when someone dies |
| IR46 | Income Tax and Corporation Tax – Clubs, Societies and Associations |
| IR51 | Business Expansion Scheme |
| IR52 | Your Tax Office – why it is where it is |
| IR56/N139 | Employed or Self-Employed? |
| IR57 | Thinking of working for yourself? |
| IR58 | Going to Work Abroad? |
| IR60 | Income Tax and Students |
| IR63 | MIRAS Mortgage Interest Relief at Source |
| IR65 | Giving to Charity – how individuals can get tax relief |
| IR74 | Deeds of Covenant – getting it right for tax |
| IR77 | Taxation of Maintenance Payments |
| IR78 | Personal Pensions |
| IR80 | Income Tax and Married Couples |
| IR82 | Independent Taxation – A Guide for Husbands on a Low Income |
| IR86 | A Guide to Mortgage Interest for Married Couples |
| IR87 | Rooms To Let |
| IR89 | Personal Equity Plans (PEPs) |
| IR90 | Independent Taxation – A Guide to Tax Allowances and Reliefs |
| IR91 | Independent Taxation – A Guide for Widows and Widowers |
| IR92 | Income Tax – A Guide for One-parent Families |
| IR93 | Separation, Divorce and Maintenance Payments |
| IR95 | Shares for Employees – Profit Sharing Schemes |
| IR97 | Shares for Employees – SAYE Share Options |
| IR103 | Tax Relief for Private Medical Insurance |
| IR110 | Can you stop paying tax on your bank and building society interest? |
| IR111 | How to claim a repayment of tax on bank and building society interest |
| IR112 | How to claim a repayment of income tax |
| IR113 | Gift Aid – A Guide for Donors and Charities |
| IR114 | TESSA – Tax Free Interest for Taxpayers |
| IR115 | Tax and Childcare |
| IR121 | Income Tax and Pensioners |
| CGT | Capital Gains Tax – An Introduction |
| CGT4 | Capital Gains Tax – Owner-occupied Houses |
| CGT6 | Capital Gains Tax – Retirement: Disposal of a business |
| CGT13 | The Indexation Allowance for Quoted Shares |
| CGT14 | Capital Gains Tax |
| CGT15 | A Guide for Married Couples |
| IHT3 | Inheritance Tax |

CHAPTER 5

# Tax Treatment of Your Investments

With few exceptions, most forms of interest are taxable and must be declared on your tax return, even if basic rate tax has been deducted at source.

If you haven't been sent a tax return and have untaxed interest to declare, it is still your legal responsibility to declare it; ring up your tax office for a tax return.

## Tax-free investments

Tax-free investments do not have to be declared on the tax return. Tax-free income includes interest on conventional and index-linked National Savings Certificates, National Savings Yearly Plan, SAYE and Premium Bond winnings. Interest on Tax Exempt Special Savings Accounts will be tax free if reinvested; if the income is withdrawn it will be paid net, but the tax withheld is paid as tax-free bonus after five years if the capital is not withdrawn before.

Tax-free income which does not have to be declared on your tax return are the dividends paid on investments in a Personal Equity Plan. There is no capital gains tax payable on the proceeds. Husband and wife can each take out one Personal Equity Plan each calendar year.

Tax-free income which does have to be declared on your tax return is the first £70 of interest from a National Savings Bank Ordinary Account. Husband and wife can each earn up to £70 a year tax free from their individual Ordinary Accounts.

The interest is declared on your tax return, because any excess over £70 which you might have earned from that account is taxable.

## Bank, Building Society, Deposit Taker and Local Authority loan and interest

Since 6 April 1991 banks, building societies, deposit takers and local authorities (in respect of their fixed term loans), all pay interest either without deduction of tax for those registered as non-taxpayers or with basic rate tax deducted at source.

It means that basic rate taxpayers have no further tax liability in respect of their investment, although it must still be declared on the tax return. However, higher rate taxpayers must pay higher rate taxes on the interest. Non-taxpayers who fail to register (forms are provided in bank and building society branches) will be able to reclaim the tax paid on their interest.

In respect of joint accounts where one partner pays tax and the other is a non-taxpayer, most building societies and some banks will pay half the interest net and the other half gross.

Older taxpayers of modest income who might qualify for Age Allowance, the extra tax relief given to those over 65, and more still to those over 75, should be careful with interest which comes "tax paid". On the tax return it has to be declared gross – that is, as though tax had not been deducted at source – in order to calculate one's total income. This is often overlooked when calculating whether or not one is entitled to the age allowance. Tax-free National Savings, such as Certificates, or Personal Equity Plans are a good investment for borderline incomes.

## To gross up "tax paid" interest

Divide the tax paid interest by 75 and multiply by 100, e.g.

**i)** Net interest of £75

$\frac{75}{75} \times 100 = £100$ gross interest

**ii)** Net interest of £100

$\frac{100}{75} \times 100 = £133$ gross interest

Higher rate taxpayers must also gross up the tax paid interest to work out their extra tax liability, e.g.

**i)** Net interest of £75 = £100 gross

A 40% rate taxpayer must pay 15% tax (i.e. 40% – 25%, the basic rate already paid) on that interest = £15 extra tax to be paid.

Net interest of £75 – £15 higher rate tax = interest net of 40% = £60.

**ii)** Net interest of £100 = £133 gross.

A 40% rate taxpayer must pay 15% more tax (i.e. 40% – 25%, the basic rate already paid) on that interest = £20 extra tax to be paid.

Net interest of £100 – £20 higher rate tax = interest net of 40% = £80.

## Inland Revenue check

Although the interest from all these forms of investment is tax paid (unless the saver is registered as a non-taxpayer), the institutions are obliged to notify the Inland Revenue where interest has been paid.

From 6 April 1992 all interest paid has to be notified to the Inland Revenue.

## National Savings Accounts, Government Stock (held on the National Savings Stock Register) and Offshore Investments which pay interest gross

The two National Savings Bank accounts (the Ordinary and Investment), National Savings Income Bonds and Pensioners Guaranteed Income Bonds, Government Stock bought from the National Savings Stock Register, War Loan, and interest from abroad is paid without deduction of tax – and these are therefore particularly appropriate forms of investment for non-taxpayers.

For taxpayers there are special rules for working out the tax on their gross interest, which depends on when they were bought. The tax is payable on 1 January of the year of assessment.

**i)** In the first tax year in which they are bought (tax years run from 6 April to the following 5 April), you are taxed on the actual interest you receive or have credited to you in that tax year. You declare the interest on your tax return for that year and will receive an assessment a few months later and be expected to pay the tax due within 30 days.

**ii)** In the second tax year, the same applies.

**iii)** In the third tax year, you are taxed on the interest you received in the *previous* year; or you can choose to pay tax on the interest you actually receive in that tax year (a worthwhile option if the interest is lower.

**iv)** In the fourth and subsequent years you pay tax on the interest you received in the previous year.

**v)** When you close an account, in that tax year you are charged tax on the actual interest you receive in that tax year.

**vi)** In the penultimate tax year, you normally pay tax on the previous year's interest (see iv above), but if you have by then closed the account, your tax assessment might be revised so that you pay tax on the actual interest received that year if it is higher.

If the amount of tax due is relatively small, the Inland Revenue might collect it by adjusting your PAYE tax code number downwards, instead of asking for a lump sum payment.

## Shares and unit trusts

Dividend income from shares and unit trusts is paid net of basic rate tax. Investors who are below the basic rate tax threshold can reclaim the tax paid, while higher rate taxpayers will have to pay the difference between basic and higher rates.

Dividend income from shares has had tax deducted at source in the form of a "tax credit" which until 5 April 1993 was at 25 per cent, the same as the basic rate of income tax. From 1993–94 onwards, the tax credit has been reduced to 20 per cent.

The change does not affect basic rate taxpayers, but higher rate taxpayers will have to pay the difference between 20 per cent and the higher rate of tax of 40 per cent on their dividend income, i.e. 20 per cent, instead of 15 per cent as before. Investors who are non-taxpayers or low taxpayers will only be able to reclaim 20 per cent.

The same situation applies to the distribution paid by unit trusts to their unitholders.

## Life insurance policies

Although life insurance companies pay tax, which affects the position of their life funds (in which your money is placed), most life insurance policy proceeds – the sum you collect at maturity or death – are free of both income and capital gains tax. The capital gains tax that life offices have to pay on their life funds is reflected in the underlying value of the investments; or with some unit-linked policies, a deduction for capital gains tax might be made from the proceeds of a policy you encash.

With investment bonds or single premium insurance bonds, higher rate taxpayers may be liable to higher rate tax *only* on the proceeds; or on the proceeds of a regular premium policy encashed before three-quarters of the original term has been reached or within 10 years (whichever is less).

Up to 5 per cent of the original investment can be withdrawn as "income" from investment bonds with the tax liability deferred until the bond is encashed or within 20 years, if earlier.

The objective for higher rate taxpayers is to defer the tax liability until a date when their tax will be lower. For both higher rate taxpayers and older taxpayers who are on the age allowance borderline, the attraction of such a plan is that the "income" does not have to be declared on the tax return.

When higher rate taxpayers encash their investment bonds, "top slicing relief" is applied to reduce the tax liability by taking into account the number of years the investment has been held.

Policyholders who took out regular premium policies before 13 March 1984 are still eligible for life assurance tax relief of 12½ per cent on the premiums. The relief is deducted from the premiums so that only the net amount is payable. Hang on to such policies, unless there are compelling reasons to stop paying.

## Personal pensions

The self-employed and those not in an occupational pension scheme have for a long time been able to build up a pension entitlement for themselves with a self-employed retirement annuity, often known as Section 226 policies. These have been replaced by personal pension plans which are available to both the self-employed and employees who do not have a company pension scheme to join, or elect not to join or remain in a company pension scheme.

Tax relief, at your highest rate, is given on personal pension plan contributions up to an earnings limit of £76,800 for entrants from 6 April 1989 onwards at the following rates:

| | |
|---|---|
| Up to age 35 | 17½% |
| Up to age 36–45 | 20% |
| Up to age 46–50 | 25% |
| Up to age 51–55 | 30% |
| Up to age 56–60 | 35% |
| 61 and over | 40% |

In addition, employees can come out of the SERPS (the State Earnings Related Pension Scheme), and the Government will invest into your personal pension plan the relevant National Insurance "contracting out" rebates for both employer and employee (currently totalling 5.8 per cent but reducing to 4.8 per cent from 1993, plus at 1 per cent age related rebate for those over 30). A 2 per cent (of earnings) bonus is paid for each year up to 1993 for all people who come out of SERPS and into a personal pension plan.

Investment is made in a tax-free investment fund, managed by a life insurance company. Other institutions such as building societies are providing personal pension plans too.

Pension investment is long term. Except for certain jobs with early "retirement" such as divers or professional sportsmen, Section 226 cannot be taken, at the moment, until age 60; with personal pension plans retirement age can be as low as 50, but few people will have earned enough to take their pension so young. The latest you can retire is 75.

Although the pension will be taxable, part of the proceeds of a personal pension plan can be taken as a lump sum, but for policies taken out after 17 March 1987, that is limited to £150,000.

Late starters who have delayed their pension planning can carry back up to six years of pension plan contributions.

Provided you have set aside the maximum amount of contribution for the current year, you can then top up the preceding tax years' contributions for a total of six years, starting with the earliest relevant year. Tax relief is given at current tax rates.

With Section 226 policies the contribution ceilings are different. There is no earnings cap.

| | |
|---|---|
| Up to age 50 | 17½% |
| Up to age 51–55 | 20% |
| Up to age 56–60 | 22½% |
| Up to age 61–75 | 27½% |

For the relevant tax years 1982–83 to 1986–87 the contribution rates were based on the year in which you were born.

| | |
|---|---|
| after 1933 | 17½% |
| 1916–1933 | 20% |
| 1914–1915 | 21% |
| 1912–1913 | 24% |
| 1910–1911 | 26½% |
| 1908–1909 | 29½% |
| 1907 or earlier | 32½% |

No tax relief is given on contributions made after age 75 years.

CHAPTER 6

# Savings and the Family

There has been a revolution in how families are taxed which has significant implications for the way we save money. Since 6 April 1990, a husband and wife have been treated as separate individuals, each with their own personal allowance. And irrespective of whether a wife's income is earned or unearned she is still able to set it against her personal allowance. (Previously, a wife's unearned income was always, from a tax point of view, treated as belonging to her husband.)

It means that from now on, each partner in the marriage is able to enjoy tax-free income of £3,445 (the level of the new personal allowance). In addition, there is the married couple's allowance of £1,720 which, in the first instance, will go to the husband but which can be transferred to the wife if his income is insufficient.

From 6 April 1994 tax relief on the married couple's allowance will be given at the 20 per cent tax rate only irrespective of the spouses' tax brackets. From April 1995 the allowance will be restricted to a 15 per cent tax rate.

In addition, each spouse is now entitled to their own capital gains tax exemption of the first £5,800 of gains in the year.

In order to maximise the family's income, it therefore makes sense to make full use of the wife's personal allowance – even if she is not working. The simplest way is to increase her savings so that she has investment income to offset against her allowance. Tax-free investments, which have hitherto been the most sensible form of investment for her, no longer fit the bill. She needs income which is either paid gross (that is before tax) or net, but on which she can reclaim any basic rate tax paid on her behalf.

For example why should she bother with a Tax Exempt Special Savings Account? She can obtain gross interest without tying up capital for five years, and she will not be able to offset the interest against her personal allowance. Similarly the tax-free income from a Personal Equity Plan will not help reduce her personal allowance.

With gross interest rates of 6–8 per cent, she can have savings of around £49,000 – and not pay tax on the interest. However, it must be from her money. If a husband gives his wife capital to invest in this tax efficient way, and the marriage subsequently fails, he cannot demand the money back. It will be hers.

Where a couple have savings in a joint name, the taxman will deem that half the interest belongs to the wife and half to the husband. If you don't want to split the income from a joint holding on a 50–50 basis, you must let the Inland Revenue know how you want it apportioned.

**Investments for Non-Working Wives**

Building Society Accounts

National Savings Investment Account
National Savings Income Bonds
High Yielding Unit Trusts
High Yielding Investment Trusts

**Investments Not Suitable for a Non-Working Wife**

National Savings Certificates
National Savings Yearly Plan
Personal Equity Plans
Tax Exempt Special Savings Account

## Children

All children are potential taxpayers and entitled to the single person's tax allowance in respect of any interest they earn, with one important exception. As they are unlikely to be taxpayers, parents should register them as non-taxpayers to receive bank or building society interest gross. Grandparents cannot do this on behalf of their grandchildren.

Income from any money given by parent(s) is, apart from the first £100, treated as the donor parent's for tax purposes. State child benefit, saved for a child, counts as a gift of money from the parent.

The one exception to the rule is when money is given to the child "absolutely" in trust, and the income accumulated until the child is 18 or marries.

So children's savings fall into two categories with the following provisos:

The increase from £5 to £100 in the amount of tax-free income from parental gifts means that the first £600 of such savings (approximately) can be invested without tax considerations.

Interest on tax-free investments are sometimes so low that they compare unfavourably with net (after tax) returns elsewhere. Parents must decide which is more important: a lower tax bill for themselves, or a better return for their children. In such circumstances, the gift could come via a non-working mother who still has some of her own personal tax allowance to use up.

**a) Savings from parental gifts**

This includes pocket money and child benefit invested on the child's behalf. The money should be in savings where the interest is tax free.

Building Society Children's Account
Bank Children's Account
Building Society Instant Access Account
National Savings Certificates
National Savings Children's Bonus Bond

**b) Savings from all other sources**

This includes birthday gifts, savings from Saturday jobs and other cash windfalls. For greatest convenience, the money should be in savings where the interest is paid gross (see above).

National Savings Bank Investment Account
National Savings Children's Bonus Bonds
Government Stock on the National Savings Stock Register
Offshore bank accounts

Alternatively, children's money can be in investments, such as shares and unit trusts, where basic rate tax is deducted at source but can be reclaimed by non-taxpayers. Use Tax Claim Form R232 to reclaim tax on behalf of a child.

Children need to learn about money management. Sometimes the investment for long-term savings which pays the most interest and has the most efficient tax structure, such as the National Savings Bank Investment Account (it requires one month's notice to withdraw funds) or the Children's Bonus Bond, might not be the most suitable for the week-to-week money transactions.

CHAPTER 7

# The Essential Savings

In Chapter One, we identified the four types of essential savings which all families should consider; single persons might be able to opt out of one of them – financial protection for dependants.

## Emergency savings

You may get no advance warning when a financial emergency strikes, so you must have money easily available to meet those unexpected bills and out-of-the-blue demands on your pocket.

The only question is how large your emergency fund should be. To a certain extent this depends on your family circumstances. A family with a chronically sick child, for example, will almost certainly need a larger emergency fund; and the self-employed will fear the cash consequences of sickness more. If you are well placed to borrow money to meet emergencies, then you might prefer to have less in your immediate emergency fund.

Between £500 and £3,000 is a suitable amount for an emergency fund. As a rule of thumb, up to three months' pay is the amount a family should consider for its emergency fund. Higher earners can probably think in terms of less; young single persons, too, will probably reduce that target. For people of modest resources, an emergency fund might be their only form of saving. If you haven't got a lump sum to earmark for emergencies, set about building one up with regular savings which carry no penalties if you have to stop saving to draw on the fund.

Because it is a fund designed for emergencies, these savings must be accessible on demand and in full. This restricts the choice to a range of bank, building society, deposit taker and offshore accounts.

In addition, the physical convenience and networks of these institutions have to be taken into account. If your emergency fund is set at quite a high level, you need not have all of it at immediate notice. Seven-day notice periods and even as long as a month's notice can be acceptable for the second tier of your emergency savings.

Do not forget that once your emergency fund has been tapped, it will either need replacing or topping up to the desired level. Bring back your second level of emergency savings to immediate access accounts, and then replace that level of savings from other sources.

## Lump sum savings immediately available

Bank Deposit Account (small penalty)
Bank High Interest Cheque Account
Bank and Deposit Taker Savings Accounts

Building Society Instant Access (provided minimum balance maintained)
Building Society Ordinary Account
Offshore High Interest Cheque Account
Offshore Single Currency Fund
National Savings Ordinary Account

## Lump sum savings available within a month

Bank High Interest Deposit Account
Bank and Deposit Taker Notice Account (some)
Building Society Notice Account (some)
National Savings Bank Investment Account
National Savings Certificates (small penalty)
National Savings Index-Linked Certificates
National Savings Premium Bond

## Regular Savings

Bank Monthly Savings Account
Building Society Monthly Savings Account

A Tax Exempt Special Savings Account (Tessa) is suitable for regular savings. Designed to be held for five years, the capital can be withdrawn earlier but you will have to sacrifice the tax-free bonus on the interest earned. If you have to dip into your Tessa for an emergency, then it becomes just like another building society account. If you are fortunate and emergencies don't strike, then your Tessa retains its tax-free benefits.

## Financial protection for your family

If you die prematurely, your wife and children will need capital and/or income to replace your earnings. If you are unable to work through ill-health or disability they will need capital and/or income to replace your savings.

Most of your savings and investments will form part of your estate and be tied up until probate (if you have made a will) or letters of administration (if you have not) has been granted.

Even more to the point, are your savings and investments sufficient to provide adequate financial protection for your dependants?

Life insurance policies, written in trust for the benefit of a man's wife (or wife's husband) and/or his (her) children, will, on the death of the policy-holder, immediately pay out the proceeds (the sum assured plus any bonuses which might have been added) without waiting for either a grant of probate or letters of administration.

The sum assured is likely to be considerably larger than your savings, particularly if you are a younger person. One guideline is that your life insurance cover should be up to five times salary, including your endowment mortgage, mortgage protection policy and any death-in-service pension scheme benefits.

Permanent health insurance policies will pay an income for the rest of your working life should you be unable to work.

The life insurance contracts discussed in the second section of the book are basically to be considered as investments, as their life insurance element is minimal.

## Saving for a house

Although it is sometimes possible to obtain a 100 per cent home loan, most people, wisely, prefer to save for a home. If mortgage funds are in short supply, regular savings will also help secure your mortgage.

*Consider:*

Bank Monthly Savings Account
Mortgage Savings Account
Building Society Monthly Savings Account

Lump sum savings towards your own home should not be locked away for longer than one month.

*Consider:*

Building Society Instant Access Account

Building Society Notice Account
Bank High Interest Deposit Account
National Savings Bank Investment Account

## Saving for retirement

Apart from the basic state pension, paid for from National Insurance contributions, everyone should now be entitled to a second pension through a company pension scheme, personal pension plan or state earnings related scheme (SERPS).

The question is whether your pension will be large enough in retirement. Many people began making their pension arrangements later in life and might not have made sufficient pension payments to look forward to a financially comfortable retirement.

With the help of your pension scheme manager, check the current day value of your future pension, and compare it with your current expenditure. If the shortfall between the two is too large today, it will almost certainly be too large when you reach retirement.

**Employees** can augment their retirement pension by:

Additional Voluntary Contributions – either to the company pension scheme, or to a "free-standing" AVC scheme of your own choice.

The **self-employed** can augment their retirement pension by:

Further contribution to a Self-Employed Retirement Annuity (taken out before 1 July 1988), or the Personal Pension Plan which succeeded it. Then carry forward contributions to top up premiums for earlier tax years.

If you want to save more than the maximum annual savings (expressed as a percentage of income) permitted to these schemes or don't wish to commit your savings irrevocably towards pensions, then consider:

Life Insurance – With-Profits Endowment Policy
Life Insurance – With-Profits Flexible Endowment Policy
Life Insurance – Unit-Linked Savings Plan
Shares – Personal Equity Plans
Shares – Unit Trust and Investment Trust Savings Plans

For lump sum investments to build up your future capital for retirement, consider:

Life Insurance – Investment Bonds
Offshore – Managed Currency Fund
Shares – Investment Trust and Unit Trust
Shares – Ordinary
Shares – Personal Equity Plans

CHAPTER 8

# Savings Strategies

## Short-term savings

Holidays, cars and weddings are three important reasons why people save; and most people have a fairly clear idea of how much they wish to spend on each.

**For holidays,** *consider:*

Bank High Interest Deposit Account
Bank High Interest Cheque Account
Building Society Instant Access Account
National Savings Bank Investment Account
Offshore High Interest Cheque Account
Offshore Single Currency Fund – for spending money

**For cars,** *consider:*

Bank Monthly Savings Account
Building Society Monthly Savings Account
Building Society Instant Access Account
National Savings Bank Investment Account

**For weddings,** *consider:*

Holidays list if the wedding is within the coming 12 months
Cars list, if the wedding is longer than 12 months away

There are inheritance tax exemptions for family gifts of money to the bride and groom (see Chapter Four).

## School fees

If you plan to educate your child privately, the earlier you start saving towards your offspring's future school fees, the better. The Assisted Places Scheme cuts the burden of school fees for less well-off parents. (Phone Independent Schools Information Service – 071–630 8793 – for more details.)

For regular savings towards future school fees needed in five or more years, consider:

Building Society SAYE
Bank or Building Society
Tax Exempt Special Savings Account
National Savings Yearly Plan
Shares – Personal Equity Plans

For savings towards school fees needed in 10 or more years, consider:

Bank or Building Society
Tax Exempt Special Savings Account
Shares – Personal Equity Plans
Shares – Unit Trust Monthly Savings Schemes
Shares – Investment Trust Monthly Savings Scheme
Life Insurance – With-Profits Flexible Policy

For lump sums for school fees, consider:

Life Insurance – Growth Bond
Life Insurance – Investment Bond
Life Insurance – School Fees Educational Trust

Shares – Unit Trusts, Investment Trusts
Stock – Government Fixed Interest, Government Index-Linked

An accumulation and maintenance trust is suitable for larger lump sums donated for the purposes of school fees by someone other than the parent, such as grandparent or godparent. There are tax advantages (see Chapter Three). A solicitor or accountant will advise you on setting up a trust.

## Divorce

Maintenance payments under a court order or enforceable separation deed made after 14 March 1988 are tax free in the hands of the recipient. Under agreements made before then, payments to a spouse above £1,720 count as taxable income; payments to a child are taxable, but the child has the single person's allowance of £3,445 to offset against it.

The payer will not be entitled to tax relief on payments made under post 14 March 1988 agreements, except up to a limit equal to the difference between the personal allowance and married couple's allowance, now £1,720. The relief will only apply at the lower, 20 per cent tax band.

If a cash settlement is made, suitable investments to provide a regular income are:

Building Society Monthly Income Account
National Savings Income Bond
Shares – Unit Trust Monthly Income Scheme

Divorce invalidates wills, widow's or widower's pension rights (unless a judge orders otherwise) and affects life insurance policies where the proceeds are in trust for a wife/husband. Both parties should check their position.

## Redundancy

Only the first £30,000 of a lump sum redundancy payment is tax free.

If you are over 50, you might be given retirement as well as redundancy and be entitled to a pension and cash commutation of your pension rights; this lump sum is also tax free.

Unemployment benefit, which lasts for up to one year, is taxable. If you are still unemployed, then you might qualify for income support, which is tax free, provided your savings do not exceed £3,000.

Whether you are planning to go into business on your own, or feel you might have to delve into your redundancy money for survival, the same rule applies: do not tie up your money for anything longer than one to three months, and be sure that you can get your money back in full. If you consider your unemployment as early retirement, look at the later sections in this chapter on retirement.

## Lump sum investments

Bank High Interest Cheque Account
Bank High Interest Deposit Account
Building Society Instant Access Account
Building Society Notice Account
National Savings Bank Investment Account
Offshore High Interest Cheque Account

## Widowhood

Widows get the widow's bereavement tax allowance of £1,720 both in the tax year of the husband's death and the following tax year too. A widow with children will also get the additional personal allowance for children. From 6 April 1994 both of these allowances can only be set against the 20 per cent tax band.

Widow's pensions and widowed mother's allowances are taxable; the child addition paid to the widow's benefit, if applicable, is tax free.

Any life insurance payable on her husband's death is tax free, even if it is paid in regular instalments as a family income benefit. A widow's pension from her husband's company pension scheme is taxable.

Some widows inherit substantial investment portfolios, and should take professional advice about them if they are inexperienced investors.

Non-working widows who are wanting monthly income should consider:

Building Society Monthly Income Account
National Savings Income Bond
National Savings Pensioners Guaranteed Income Bond (if over 65 years old)

and for future growth:

Shares – Unit Trust Monthly Income Plan

## Retirement

The extra tax allowance for those over 65 and on modest incomes needs careful planning.

Anyone over 65 is entitled to the personal age allowance of £4,200. The married couple's allowance of £2,665 goes initially to the husband. If he is under 65 and his wife over 65, special arrangements are made.

When your income exceeds £14,200, the extra age allowance is reduced by £1 for every £2 of income until it is finally extinguished and you are on the normal tax allowance level. For the individual, this occurs when income reaches £15,710, for the person claiming the married couple's allowance it is £17,600.

There is an extra age allowance of £4,370 (personal) and £2,705 (married) for those over 75. The income limit remains £14,200; therefore the extra age allowance is reduced by £1 for every £2 of income until it is extinguished at £16,050 (personal), £17,680 (including married couple's allowance).

It is important to keep your income under the threshold of £14,200 if you are a borderline case, and look for income which does not have to be declared on your tax return.

*Consider:*

Bank or Building Society – Tax Exempt Special Savings Account
Life Assurance – Investment Bond 5 per cent withdrawal plan
National Savings Certificates – cashing units each year to provide an "income" and leaving your capital intact
Shares – Personal Equity Plan

Do not forget to gross up the interest paid by banks, building societies, deposit takers and local authorities in calculating your total income. If your total income is near the £14,200 level, the gross interest could result in some lost personal allowance. See Chapter Five.

Retirement can last a long time, and although more and more company pensions are increasing payments, it is not wise (if you have sufficient capital for a spread of investment) to have the rest of your retirement savings entirely in fixed capital investments. Interest rates can go down.

*Consider:*

Bank and Building Society – Tax Exempt Special Savings Account
Building Society Instant Access
Bank High Interest Cheque Account
Offshore High Interest Account
National Savings Income Bonds
National Savings Pensioners Guaranteed Income Bond (if over 65 years old)
Shares – Unit Trust – Monthly Income Plan
Shares – Investment Trusts

## Very old

Annuities begin to look attractive for men and women in their seventies. Home income plans, a way of boosting retirement income by using the capital tied up in your own home, are available to individuals over 70 and married couples with a joint age of 150 years.

CHAPTER 9

# Investor Protection

There are two kinds of risk facing the investor.

Investment risk is the possibility of losing some, even all, of your money in an asset which fluctuates in value (see Chapter Two).

The other kind of risk investors take is that the body or institution looking after their money might go bust; or that the person or organisation handling your investments might go bust or fail to invest your money for you.

Various safeguards exist to protect investors from such eventualities, however unlikely they might be in some cases. And if the worst were to happen, compensation schemes will provide some financial consolation.

## Financial Services Act

This major piece of investor protection legislation came into force in stages in 1988.

The Securities and Investments Board (SIB) has the power through satellite Self-Regulatory Organisations (SROs) to vet all investment businesses.

There are well-established plans to set up a Personal Investment Authority (PIA) in 1994 which will take over the regulation of all retail investments and encompass the work of LAUTRO and FIMBRA. Meantime, the SROs which most concern the private investor are:

**Financial Intermediaries, Managers and Brokers Regulatory Association (FIMBRA)** covers insurance brokers and other financial intermediaries giving independent financial advice.

**Life Assurance and Unit Trust Regulatory Organisation (LAUTRO)** covers organisations selling life insurance and unit trusts.

**Investment Managers Regulatory Organisation (IMRO)** covers all investment management organisations such as unit trust, investment trust, pension fund and life insurance fund management.

**The Securities & Futures Authority (SFA)** covers stockbrokers and securities dealers and now includes the Association of Futures Brokers and Dealers.

It is a criminal offence to carry on an investment business without authorisation from either the SIB or the appropriate SRO.

The SIB holds a complete list of authorised firms or individuals. Make sure that your investment adviser, fund manager or stockbroker is authorised by calling 071–929 3652. You will be told the firm's full name, head office address, which SRO it is authorised by and the areas of business the firm is authorised to deal in.

Each SRO has established a complaints procedure to assist investors with a grievance. In addition, each has appointed an ombudsman or referee to deal impartially with investors' complaints which the normal procedure has not resolved. The ombudsmen have the power to make financial awards in the case of maladministration, etc. They do not investigate a disappointing investment performance.

The telephone numbers for the four SROs with which you are likely to have the most contact are:

FIMBRA: 071–538 8860
LAUTRO: 071–379 0444
IMRO: 071–628 6022
SFA: 071–378 9000

In the event of an authorised investment business failing, the Financial Services Act provides some measure of compensation.

**The SIB Compensation Scheme** covers 100 per cent of the first £30,000 of savings and 90 per cent of the next £20,000, an overall maximum compensation of £48,000.

Individual SROs' compensation schemes mirror the SIB's.

There are other compensation schemes available to investors. These are:

**Banks and deposit takers** are both classified as "authorised institutions" by the Bank of England. The level of compensation is up to 75 per cent of the first £20,000 of deposits.

Banking activity which needs authorisation under the Financial Services Act is covered by the compensation scheme of the appropriate SRO.

The Banking Ombudsman (tel: 071–404 9944) will investigate complaints that normal banking complaints procedures fail to solve.

**Building societies** are exempt from the SIB or SROs' compensation schemes, but societies' own statutory compensation schemes covers 90 per cent of savings up to £20,000.

The Building Societies Ombudsman (tel: 071–931 0044) will deal with intractable complaints.

**UK authorised insurance companies** are covered by the Policyholders Protection Act providing 90 per cent of policy benefits, provided these are not "excessive". This compensation scheme remains in force. The Insurance Ombudsman (tel: 071–928 4488) has limited powers to investigate life assurance contracts in the case of an intractable dispute.

**Unit trusts** no longer have their own individual Ombudsman, but come under the wing of the Insurance Ombudsman (tel: 071–928 4488).

**National Savings** are guaranteed by the Government.

CHAPTER 10

# Banks and Deposit Takers*

## Cash Card Account

Cash card accounts offer an easy withdrawal and deposit system through the hole-in-the-wall cash machines and other cash dispensers or automated teller machines (ATMs). They usually pay higher rates of interest than interest-bearing current accounts. Other services are often included such as standing orders and mini statements.

**Suitable for** Salary transfers, day-to-day money management for cash, rather than for cheque-book-oriented customers. Also for older children who do not need or want a cheque book facility.

**Open to** Anyone usually over 16.

**Min–Max** £1; no maximum.

**Charges** None.

**Withdrawals** Up to £100–£250 a day in cash from ATMs.

**Interest** Variable; usually paid half-yearly or annually. Rates are tiered so that the more you have, the more you earn.

* *Both are classified as "authorised institutions" under The Banking Act 1987.*

**Tax** Interest is added net of basic rate tax; higher rate taxpayers must pay more. Banks can pay interest gross to non-taxpayers; non-taxpayers who fail to register will still be able to reclaim the basic rate tax deducted at source.

**Children** Yes.

**How to invest** At your local branch including Barclays, National Westminster and Yorkshire.

**Record** Regular statements.

**Money Mail Rating** *****

**Investor protection** Bank savings compensation scheme covers 75 per cent of savings up to £20,000 with a maximum payout of £15,000 per person.

**Comment** Compare facilities and rates with accounts offered by building societies. The Lloyds account is aimed at the higher end of the market and makes a monthly charge if the balance falls below £1,000. National Westminster's First Reserve, aimed at first-time savers, offers competitive rates of interest for a low level of savings.

# Children's Account

Children's bank accounts may offer a range of free gifts and magazines. Some banks now have a separate account for older children and young people with a cash dispenser card. Midland, TSB and Yorkshire are the most active banks on the school banking scene.

**Suitable for** Children's pocket money and encouraging money management.

**Open to** Children up to 16, occasionally 14. Thereafter account reverts to deposit or cash card account.

**Min–Max** Ranges from £1–£10; no maximum.

**Withdrawals** Either seven days' notice (or loss of seven days' interest if immediate) or immediate withdrawal. Instant cash dispenser withdrawals allowed in most cases for young people over 13 years.

**Interest** Variable; usually paid half-yearly into account. Banks can pay interest gross to non-taxpayers.

**Children** Yes, but parent's signature is required for withdrawals for under-sevens.

**How to invest** Apply at a bank branch. Obtain form to register child as non-taxpayer from branch. Only parents can sign on behalf of a child.

**Record** Half-yearly statements and paying-in books.

**Money Mail Rating** *****

**Investor protection** Bank savings compensation scheme covers 75 per cent of savings up to £20,000. Maximum payout £15,000 per person.

**Comment** Convenience, including a Saturday morning branch (as banking hours do not fit in with school hours), and highest available interest rate should be just as important as the free gifts, money boxes and magazines!

Check whether your local building society children's schemes offer a higher rate of interest; the gifts will be less impressive. For larger sums, consider money which can be "locked up", possibly with a higher interest rate.

# Deposit Account

Basic bank interest-bearing account requiring seven days' notice to withdraw funds or loss of seven days' interest if withdrawn immediately. No cheque book.

| | |
|---|---|
| Suitable for | Lump sums below the threshold for High Interest Deposit Account, but not recommended. |
| Open to | Anyone. |
| Min–Max | £1 minimum; no maximum. |
| Withdrawals | Any amount at seven days' notice, or immediately with loss of seven days' interest. |
| Interest | Variable, usually paid half-yearly either to this account or current account. |
| Tax | Interest is paid net of tax; higher rate taxpayers pay more. Banks can pay interest gross to non-taxpayers. |
| Children | Yes, but Bank Children's Account a better investment. |
| How to invest | At any branch of most banks. You need not have a current account with the bank. Register at branch to obtain gross interest. |
| Record | Usually none. Half-yearly statement. Keep paying-in slip stubs. |
| Money Mail Rating | ***** |
| Investor protection | Bank savings compensation scheme covers 75 per cent of savings up to £20,000. |
| Comment | It is hard to make a case for investing in a Bank Deposit Account which pays the lowest rate of interest of all bank accounts, and less than building society ordinary account. Non-taxpayers should consider a National Savings Investment Account. |

# High Interest Cheque Account

Interest-bearing current account, usually with minimum starting investment, often £2,000–£2,500. It is a cheque-book account, but some banks stipulate minimum cheque withdrawal of £200–£250. Standing orders and overdrafts are allowed; sometimes run primarily in conjunction with group's investment management arm. Credit card facility often included.

| | |
|---|---|
| Suitable for | Investors with frequent high value transactions such as school fees and large household bills; bank customers who habitually keep too much in their current account or keep household running funds in an interest-bearing but less flexible building society account. |
| Open to | Anyone aged 18 or over. |
| Min–Max | Minimum commonly £2,000–£2,500, but can be as low as £500. No maximum. |
| Charges | In most cases none. If balance with Save & Prosper account drops below a set level, there is a charge of £5 a month; limited number of free cheques at some banks. |
| Withdrawals | Sometimes minimum cheque withdrawal of £200–£250, but most groups have no minimum cheque withdrawals. Where a credit card is part of the package, monthly repayment can be below minimum cheque level. |
| Interest | Variable, calculated daily; sometimes a tiered rate so larger amounts earn more. Make sure you keep the minimum opening balance in the account or you will get a very low interest rate. |
| Tax | Interest is paid net of tax; higher rate taxpayers pay more. Banks can pay interest gross to non-taxpayers; non-taxpayers who fail to register as such will still be able to reclaim the basic rate tax deducted at source. |
| Children | Not unless account held in adult's name. |

**How to invest** Apply in writing or through branch network to Abbey National, Allied Trust Bank, Bank of Ireland, Bank of Scotland, Barclays, Caledonian Bank, Cater Allen, Clydesdale, Kleinwort Benson, Lloyds, Midland, National Westminster, Royal Bank of Scotland, Save & Prosper (Robert Fleming), Schroder, Tyndall, Western Trust.

**Record** Bank statement, usually quarterly.

**Money Mail Rating** *****

**Investor protection** Bank savings compensation scheme covers 75 per cent of savings up to £20,000. Maximum payout £15,000 per person.

**Comment** Without a cheque guarantee card, it is hard to see this account really overthrowing the bank current account, even when it is used extensively in conjunction with a credit card for retail purchases. But with full banking facilities – cheque guarantee card, standing order payments and overdrafts – it can replace the current account entirely.

# Instant Access Account

An easy access high interest account, with a minimum balance of often at least £1,000, frequently with a tiered interest rate structure so that larger amounts earn more. A monthly income facility is sometimes included.

**Suitable for** Lump sum investments for emergencies, day-to-day money management, irregular savings, "rainy day" money.

**Open to** Anyone.

**Min–Max** £500–£2,000 minimum; no maximum.

**Charges** None.

**Withdrawals** On demand from any branch.

**Interest** Variable, usually tiered so that larger sums earn more, paid quarterly or annually. Rates are usually higher than a High Interest Cheque Account.

**Tax** Interest is paid net of tax; higher rate taxpayers pay more. Banks can pay interest gross to non-taxpayers; non-taxpayers who fail to fill in the self-certification form will still be able to reclaim the basic rate tax deducted at source.

**Children** Yes, but parent's signature for withdrawals for under-sevens.

**How to invest** At branch or apply in writing to Abbey National, Allied Trust, Barclays, Clydesdale, Co-operative Bank, First Direct, Girobank, Lloyds, Midland, National Westminster, Royal Bank of Scotland, TSB, Tyndall.

**Record** Bank statement.

**Money Mail Rating** *****

**Investor protection** Bank savings compensation scheme covers 75 per cent of savings up to £20,000. Maximum payout £15,000 per person.

**Comment** Much better than an ordinary deposit account; always compare rates with building society instant access accounts. National Westminster First Reserve, aimed at first-time savers, has a minimum opening balance of just £1 and gives a cash card.

# Interest-Bearing Current Account

In the wake of increased competition from building societies, most of the High Street banks have launched one or more current accounts which pay interest. Such an account should not be viewed as an investment.

**Suitable for** Day-to-day money management for people who habitually keep their current accounts in credit.

**Open to** Anyone over 18.

**Min–Max** £1; no maximum.

**Charges** Free if account in credit. Often a monthly or quarterly fee for overdrawn customers.

**Withdrawals** On demand.

**Interest** Variable, and often tiered so that large balances earn more.

**Tax** Interest is paid net of tax; higher rate taxpayers will pay more. Banks can pay interest gross to non-taxpayers; non-taxpayers who fail to register will still be able to reclaim the basic rate tax deducted at source.

**Children** No, if automatic loan facilities are included in the account package. Children's savings accounts can be converted later.

**How to invest** At any branch of most banks.

**Record** Regular statements.

**Money Mail Rating** *****

**Investor protection** Bank compensation scheme covers 75 per cent of credit balances up to £20,000. Maximum payout £15,000 per person.

**Comment** Rates vary, so choose a bank with the best rate for your likely balance. Charges can be high if overdrawn over a certain limit, usually £100–£250, so these accounts are more suitable for individuals who retain a credit balance each month rather than going into the red.

# Monthly Income Account

Lump sum investment, which can usually be increased at any time, which pays higher rate interest monthly into the customer's current account. Withdrawal notice period varies from none to one year according to the account to which the facility is linked.

**Suitable for** Those needing to boost monthly income who have a current or other account for day-to-day money management.

**Open to** Anyone.

**Min–Max** £1,000–£2,500 minimum; no maximum.

**Charges** None.

**Withdrawals** Withdrawals after notice period if any.

**Interest** Variable, paid monthly. Rates are tiered so that the more you invest, the more you earn; rates are substantially better for those with £10,000 or more. Abbey National, Allied Trust and First Direct normally pay competitive rates.

**Tax** Interest is paid net of tax; higher rate taxpayers pay more. Banks can pay interest gross to non-taxpayers; non-taxpayers who fail to register will still be able to reclaim the basic rate tax deducted at source.

**Children** Not suitable.

**How to invest** At any branch of most banks.

**Record** Regular statements.

**Money Mail Rating** *****

**Investor protection** Bank savings compensation scheme covers 75 per cent of savings up to £20,000. Maximum payout £15,000 per person.

**Comment** Always compare rates with building society monthly income accounts and the National Savings Income Bond.

# Monthly Savings Account

Regular monthly savings scheme for unlimited period. Your level of savings can be varied after six months and you can miss one month's savings without penalty. If savings cease, the account reverts to a deposit account.

**Suitable for** Regular savings of small amounts; short-term savings such as for a holiday or specific purchase; first-time savers.

**Open to** Anyone.

**Min–Max** £10 a month minimum; usually no maximum.

**Charges** None.

**Withdrawals** Withdrawal usually permitted once every six months.

**Interest** Variable; paid half-yearly in most cases either to this account or a current account.

**Tax** Interest is paid net of tax; higher rate taxpayers pay more. Banks can pay interest gross to non-taxpayers; non-taxpayers who fail to register will still be able to reclaim the basic rate tax deducted at source.

**Children** Yes; investments in a child's name cannot be withdrawn by under-sevens.

**How to invest** Apply at a branch of any bank; you need not have a current account with the bank.

**Record** Half-yearly or annual statements.

**Money Mail Rating** *****

**Investor protection** Bank savings compensation scheme covers 75 per cent of savings up to £20,000. Maximum payout £15,000 per person.

**Comment** There are small interest-rate variations on this account at different banks. Girobank pays a competitive rate. Compare with bank and building society instant access accounts with a low minimum opening balance of £1 such as National Westminster First Reserve and Nationwide Cashbuilder.

# Notice Account

Lump sum investment which requires notice of one, two, three or six months to withdraw funds. Investors have the option of losing interest for relevant period and instant access on funds.

**Suitable for** Relatively short-term "parking" of money not immediately required nor considered as part of your emergency money.

**Open to** Anyone.

**Min–Max** £100–£500 minimum. £25,000–£50,000 maximum.

**Charges** None.

**Withdrawals** Partial or full withdrawals permitted after specified notice period, or you can accept loss of interest if you withdraw before then. If you keep a balance, usually of £10,000, instant withdrawal from the surplus is usually allowed without penalty. National Westminster allows £250 a month withdrawal without penalty.

**Interest** Variable, usually paid half-yearly or quarterly. It can be paid by cheque, or direct into a bank account, or reinvested.

**Tax** Interest is paid net of tax; higher rate taxpayers pay more. Banks can pay interest gross to non-taxpayers; non-taxpayers who fail to register will still be able to reclaim the basic rate tax deducted at source.

**Children** Yes; parent's signature normally required for under-sevens.

**How to invest** Check interest rates at a local branch.

**Investor protection** Bank savings compensation scheme covers 75 per cent of savings up to £20,000. Maximum payout £15,000 per person.

**Comment** In general bank savings rates have become much more competitive in recent years. Compare interest rates and the minimum investment required with building society instant access accounts. Abbey National offers good 90 days' notice account, TSB 60 days' notice; and Barclays and National Westminster one month's notice.

# Save As You Earn (SAYE)

2nd Issue

Regular monthly savings scheme for five years with an option to leave your investment for a further two years. Interest, which accumulates, is tax free and in addition there is a bonus equivalent to 14 months' payments, tax free, at the end of five years, or 28 months' tax-free payments if you leave the savings in for the next two years. A gap of six months' savings can be made up.

**Suitable for** Higher rate taxpayers, regular savings for an unspecified purpose, particularly when interest rates are falling.

**Open to** Anyone aged 16 or over who does not have a SAYE account elsewhere.

**Min–Max** £1 a month minimum; £20 maximum.

**Charges** None.

**Withdrawals** No partial withdrawals; repayment takes two to three weeks. Reduced interest rate penalties on early withdrawals: no interest in year one, years two to five interest of 6 per cent only (8 per cent if you die).

**Interest** Fixed. Including the bonus, the rate is equivalent to 8.3 per cent a year over five years; including the enlarged bonus, the rate over seven years is equivalent to 8.62 per cent a year. It accumulates and is paid out when the contract matures.

**Tax** Tax free.

**Children** No.

**How to invest** Apply at bank branches.

**Record** Certificate.

**Money Mail Rating** *****

**Investor protection** Bank savings compensation scheme covers 75 per cent of savings up to £20,000.

**Comment** All banks will offer identical terms, so convenience is the main yardstick. Be sure you can keep up the savings for five years; early surrender rates are unattractive.

# Save As You Earn (SAYE)

Series "F" Share Option Scheme

Regular monthly savings linked to a company share option scheme. Employees are offered the option to buy shares at a price fixed at the start of the five-year savings period which cannot be less than 80 per cent of their market value. Employees invest a set amount each month in the SAYE scheme. At the end of five years they can either use the money to exercise the share option or take the money with a bonus. They can leave the money invested for another two years to obtain a higher bonus BUT they will then lose the share option entitlement. However, some employers offer a seven-year share option plan when the share option can then be exercised.

Interest in the SAYE accumulates tax free. In addition there is a bonus of 9 months' payments tax free at the end of five years, or 18 months' if you leave the savings in for the next two years.

**Suitable for** Employees who want to build up a share stake in their company.

**Open to** Employers running a scheme fix the eligibility rules, usually determined by length of service with the company. Employees may have more than one share option SAYE scheme, provided the overall monthly contribution does not exceed the maximum.

**Min–Max** £10 a month minimum; £250 maximum.

**Charges** None.

**Withdrawals** No partial withdrawals. Reduced interest rate penalties on early withdrawal; no interest in year one, years two to five, 5 per cent only. If you die, your executor can either take the amount saved or buy shares at the option price.

**Interest** Fixed. Including the bonus is equivalent to 5.3 per cent over five years; including the enlarged bonus, the rate over seven years is equivalent to 5.87 per cent. It is accumulated.

**Tax** Tax free. Once the share option is exercised, dividends are taxable and there is a potential gains tax liability, based on the actual purchase price of the shares, when you sell them.

**Children** No.

**How to invest** You will be invited to participate by your employer who must have Inland Revenue approval for the scheme.

**Record** Certificate.

**Money Mail Rating** ***** until the share option is exercised.

**Investor protection** Bank compensation scheme covers 75 per cent of savings up to £20,000. Maximum payout £15,000 per person.

**Comment** A useful way of hedging your bets. If the company's share rise has risen since you were granted the option, then you exercise the option and buy the share at the lower price fixed when you began savings. You will have a built-in profit. However, if your company has been less successful and the share price is actually lower than the option price, then take the SAYE proceeds as cash.

# Tax Exempt Special Savings Account

Tessa, for short, is a new form of saving available since the beginning of 1991. It is a five year account for either regular or irregular lump savings and provided the capital is left intact for five years, the interest is tax free. If the interest is withdrawn before then, it will be paid net of basic rate tax, but the amount reserved for tax will be paid as a tax-free bonus at the end of the five year period. If the capital is withdrawn before, the interest is taxable.

**Suitable for** Erratic lump sum savers, taxpayers and "rainy day" savings.

**Open to** Anyone over 18.

**Min–Max** Overall maximum over five years, £9,000. Maximum per month £150. Maximum lump sums of £3,000 in year one, £1,800 in years two to four, £600 in year five.

**Charges** None.

**Withdrawals** Interest can be taken net within the five year period. Capital can be withdrawn at any time, but the tax advantages will be lost.

**Interest** Variable, usually annual. Confederation Bank offers fixed rate scheme.

**Tax** Interest is tax free provided capital is not withdrawn early. If net interest is taken during the five year span, the amount reserved for tax will be paid as a tax-free bonus at the end of the term.

**Children** No.

**Record** Initial certificate and annual update.

**Money Mail Rating** *****

**Comment** An attractive and flexible savings vehicle, suitable for second line emergency savings. Tessas may be transferred from one deposit taker to another but this may entail a loss of bonus or a charge. Not all providers allow transfers into their schemes. Compare with rates offered by building societies. Pick a plan with attractive rates but with no penalties on transfer out.

# Term Account

Lump sum, fixed interest rate investment with money tied up from one month to five years. The interest rate does not necessarily vary with the length of the investment. Variable rate schemes are also available.

**Suitable for** Anyone taking a view that interest rates elsewhere will fall soon and who wants to lock into fixed rates.

**Open to** Anyone.

**Min–Max** Minimum commonly £2,000, but can be as little as £500 or as much as £5,000. Usually no maximum.

**Charges** None.

**Withdrawals** At end of term, other than in exceptional circumstances, but if so the interest rate is usually reduced.

**Interest** Fixed higher rates are sometimes negotiable for larger sums. Although fixed for the term, the rates quoted for new deposits change in line with other bank interest rates. For shorter-term investments interest is payable at maturity, otherwise half-yearly or annually.

**Tax** Interest is paid net of tax; higher rate taxpayers pay more. Banks can pay interest gross to non-taxpayers; non-taxpayers who fail to register will still be able to reclaim the basic rate tax deducted at source.

**Children** Not suitable.

**How to invest** Interest rates are quoted in bank branches and newspaper advertisements (deposit takers). Apply at a branch, or in writing.

**Record** Statement.

**Money Mail Rating** *****

**Investor protection** Bank savings compensation scheme covers 75 per cent of savings up to £20,000.

**Comment** Locking up your money at a fixed rate of interest for a long period is usually inadvisable because of the loss of flexibility. But when interest rates are exceptionally high they could be a bargain. Compare returns with guaranteed income bonds over the same investment time span. Abbey National offers variable rate term shares.

CHAPTER 11

# Building Societies

## Cash Card Account

Cash card accounts, operating through the LINK network, offer an easy withdrawal and deposit system via hole-in-the-wall cash machines and other cash dispensers or automated teller machines (ATMs). Other services, such as standing orders and mini statements, are available in some cases. Originally introduced as an alternative to a cheque book account, in practice more and more societies are adding cheque book facilities to cash card accounts.

| | |
|---|---|
| Suitable for | Salary transfers. Day-to-day money management for cash, rather than cheque-book oriented customers. Older children, particularly the technology minded. |
| Open to | Anyone over age 13, sometimes 16. |
| Min-Max | £1 minimum; no maximum. |
| Charges | None. |
| Withdrawals | Up to £100–£250 a day cash from ATMs; larger cheque withdrawals at counter. |
| Interest | Variable. Account can be tied into either ordinary or instant access accounts and their interest rates and tiers, if relevant, apply. Interest is usually paid half-yearly or annually and accumulated. |

**Tax** Interest is paid net of tax; higher rate taxpayers must pay more. Building societies can pay interest gross to non-taxpayers; non-taxpayers who fail to register will still be able to reclaim the basic rate tax deducted at source.

**Children** Yes, over age 13–16.

**How to invest** At a local branch. Larger societies offering this account include Alliance & Leicester, Birmingham Midshires, Bradford & Bingley, Bristol & West, Derbyshire, Halifax.

**Record** Passbook if tied to another account, otherwise regular statements (which can be updated at the ATM).

**Money Mail Rating** *****

**Investor protection** Building society savings compensation scheme covers 90 per cent of savings up to £20,000. Maximum payout £18,000 per depositor.

**Comment** Building societies have pushed this account hard as an alternative to much more expensive to administer (from their point of view) cheque book facilities, but are increasingly offering both. Direct debiting from the card account in stores is a development to watch. Alliance & Leicester offers telephone banking service through its "Cash Plus" account.

# Cheque Book Account

Several large societies offer a full cheque-book banking service, including a cheque guarantee card, complete with current account interest. Other societies run cheque book accounts but not with full banking facilities (see High Interest Cheque Accounts). Some of the existing cheque book accounts neither permit overdrafts nor have a cheque guarantee card, but do usually have a credit card link.

**Suitable for** Cheque book accounts are becoming increasingly competitive with a bank current account and charges tend to be lower.

**Open to** Anyone aged 18 or over.

**Min–Max** Varies from £1 minimum up to £100,000 maximum.

**Charges** Cheques are usually free unless the account drops below minimum balance, if required. Charges for bounced or stopped cheques. Overdraft interest.

**Withdrawals** By cheque, cash on demand up to £250, cash withdrawal machine.

**Interest** Variable, and sometimes tiered so that the more you have in your account, the more you earn. Interest is usually paid yearly. Northern Rock pay monthly.

**Tax** Interest is paid net of tax; higher rate taxpayers pay more. Building societies can pay interest gross to non-taxpayers; non-taxpayers who fail to register will still be able to reclaim the basic rate tax deducted at source.

**How to invest** At branches of Britannia, Chelsea, Halifax, Nationwide, Northern Rock, North of England, Norwich & Peterborough and Woolwich.

**Record** Passbook and cheque book stub for additional reference or a monthly bank statement and no passbook.

**Money Mail Rating** *****

**Investor protection** Building society compensation scheme covers 90 per cent of savings up to £20,000. Maximum payout £18,000 per person.

**Comment** Accounts need to be run in conjunction with a credit card to be really effective. Accounts are fully competitive and should be compared with bank interest-bearing current accounts. Which suits you best depends on how you run your financial affairs. Among the building societies Britannia, Chelsea and Northern Rock usually offer good rates.

# Children's Account

Incentive account to attract young people into becoming savers with the help of favourite cartoon characters, gifts, comics, badges, pens and money boxes. Most societies pay their junior members more than the ordinary account rate. There are different accounts for different ages, generally up to 11, and 11 and over.

**Suitable for** Pocket money and lump sums and teaching children how to manage their own savings.

**Open to** Children up to a stipulated age, most commonly 16 or 18 but sometimes as low as 10. A handful of societies have a lower age limit of five.

**Min–Max** £1 minimum; no maximum.

**Charges** None.

**Withdrawals** On demand from any branch up to £250 cash, cheques up to £5,000. Parent's signature required for withdrawals under the age of seven, occasionally until a child reaches age 10 or 12.

**Interest** Variable with wide variations in rates. Some pay a narrow margin over the miserly ordinary share rate while others are much more generous. Interest paid annually or half-yearly and accumulates.

**Tax** Building societies can pay interest gross to non-taxpayers, including children. Children must be registered as non-taxpayers by their parents. Forms available in branches.

**How to invest** Over 40 societies, including all the major ones, run Children's Accounts. Apply at a local branch.

**Record** Passbook. Britannia runs a cash card account for age 11 plus.

**Money Mail Rating** *****

**Investor protection** Building society compensation scheme covers 90 per cent of savings up to £20,000. Maximum payout £18,000 per person.

**Comment** Convenience for school or Saturday leisure activities is the most important aspect of a children's account, and in this respect the building society still scores over the children's bank account which is inaccessible on weekdays during term time. Money-wise kids will appreciate higher interest rates more than the "freebies". Parents should watch the tax trap if money they give to their offspring is invested in a children's account. Tax-free National Savings Certificates or Children's Bonus Bonds would be more appropriate for their regular or substantial money gifts.

Britannia offers an attractive account with good rates of interest (with card and passbook) for those aged 11–15. Melton Mowbray's Sunny Bond has earned a reputation for good rates for the serious saver (£250 minimum).

# Instant Access Account

Building society premium account offering high rates of interest, often on a tiered basis so that the more you invest, the more you earn. A monthly income facility is sometimes included. See also Postal Accounts.

**Suitable for** Lump sum investments, particularly emergency funds; irregular savings; salary transfers and day-to-day money management.

**Open to** Anyone.

**Min–Max** £500–£1,000, occasionally as little as £1. No maximum.

**Charges** None.

**Withdrawals** On demand from any branch, usually up to £250 in cash, £5,000–£15,000 by cheque.

**Interest** Variable. Rates are tiered so higher balances earn more. Large sums earn 1¼–1¾ per cent more than smaller amounts. If the balances drops below minimum level then the ordinary share rate is payable. Interest is usually paid annually, to be accumulated, or paid by cheque or direct into bank or building society account. Monthly income is sometimes available and may be at a slightly lower rate of interest.

**Tax** Interest is paid net of tax; higher rate taxpayers pay more. Building societies can pay interest gross to non-taxpayers; non-taxpayers who fail to register will still be able to reclaim the basic rate of tax deducted at source.

**Children** Yes, but parent's signature is required for under-sevens.

**How to invest** Apply at a branch or agency. Postal service is frequently available.

**Record** Passbook.

**Money Mail Rating** *****

**Investor protection** Building society savings compensation scheme covers 90 per cent of savings up to £20,000. Maximum payout £18,000 per person.

**Comment** A flexible and versatile account which permits easy switching of funds for those very interested in rates. Check carefully where the trigger points are for the higher interest payments: the first can be as high as £5,000 instead of the more common, and more easily attainable, £2,500. Interest paid half-yearly has a higher compound annual rate if you reinvest the interest. For smaller savers Portman (minimum £500) pays good rates. Alliance & Leicester and National & Provincial are also usually competitive.

# High Interest Cheque Account

Interest bearing current account, with a minimum starting sum of £2,000 or £2,500, offered by a handful of societies. Account holders get a cheque book and usually a cash card, cheque guarantee card but no overdraft facility. Standing orders and direct debit facilities are usually available. The interest rate drops dramatically if your balance falls below the usual minimum.

**Suitable for** Investors with frequent high value transactions such as school fees and large household bills.

**Open to** Anyone aged 18 or over.

**Min–Max** Commonly £2,000–£2,500.

**Charges** None.

**Withdrawals** By cheque or hole-in-the-wall machines with the cash card. Halifax stipulates a minimum cheque withdrawal of £200 and does not offer a cash card.

**Interest** Variable and added monthly, quarterly or annually depending on the account. The rates are usually tiered so that the more you have in your account, the more you earn. Expect a derisory rate if your balance falls below the minimum opening balance.

**Tax** Interest is paid net of basic rate tax; higher rate taxpayers pay more. Building societies can pay interest gross to non-taxpayers. Non-taxpayers who fail to register will still be able to reclaim the basic rate tax deducted at source.

**Children** No.

**How to invest** Apply to High Street branches. Large building societies offering this type of account include Bristol & West, Chelsea, Halifax and Portman.

**Record** Statement, usually quarterly.

**Money Mail Rating** *****

**Investor protection** Building society savings compensation scheme covers 90 per cent of savings up to £20,000. Maximum payout £18,000 per person.

**Comment** Compare with current accounts on offer from banks and make sure the account is flexible enough to meet your needs. Chelsea runs its Classic Account through the post. Halifax Asset Reserve Account, where interest rates are linked to wholesale money market rates, has a higher than usual minimum balance of £5,000 and a minimum cheque withdrawal of £200.

# Monthly Income Account

Lump sum investment which pays interest monthly and which is usually linked to either an instant access, notice account or term account (see pages **55** and **59**). Some societies pay the same rates of interest in which case the compound annual rate (CAR) is higher; others trim the interest marginally because it is paid monthly.

**Suitable for** Retired persons (but check the age allowance trap, see page **31**) and others, such as non-working mothers, who need monthly income.

**Open to** Anyone.

**Min–Max** £2,000–£2,500 although occasionally lower. No maximum.

**Charges** None.

**Withdrawals** Same as for underlying account.

**Interest** Variable, paid monthly either by cheque or direct to bank or other building society account. Halifax offers a fixed rate for one year.

**Tax** Interest paid net of tax; higher rate taxpayers pay more. Gross interest available for registered non-taxpayers.

**Children** Not suitable.

**How to invest** Most societies have monthly income accounts. Apply at a branch. Postal service is frequently available.

**Record** Passbook; half-yearly or annual statements as well in some cases.

**Money Mail Rating** *****

**Investor protection** Building society savings compensation scheme covers 90 per cent of savings up to £20,000. Maximum payout £18,000 per person.

**Comment** Shop around: interest rates and thresholds for higher interest rates on tiered accounts vary. Check the compound annual rate (CAR), particularly if you plan to reinvest rather than spend the income. Compare with National Savings Income Bonds, Pensioners Guaranteed Income Bond (for ages 65 and over) and Guaranteed Income Bonds. Top rates from building societies are usually available on term shares but instant access postal accounts run by Bradford & Bingley and Cheltenham & Gloucester offer good rates.

## Notice Account

Lump sum investment account which requires notice of from seven days to one, two or three months to withdraw funds. With accounts needing notice of one month or more, investors have the option of loss of interest for relevant period and instant access. Accounts are usually tiered so that the more you have invested, the more you earn. Monthly income is usually available.

**Suitable for** Lump sum investments needed at a specific future date and longer-term investments.

**Open to** Anyone.

**Min–Max** £500–£1,000 minimum; no maximum.

**Charges** None.

**Withdrawals** Any amount after required notice period, or instant access if you accept loss of interest for relevant notice period. This option is not always available on seven day notice accounts. If you keep a balance, usually of £10,000, instant withdrawal from the surplus is allowed.

**Interest** Variable, usually paid annually to be accumulated or paid by cheque or direct into another account, or paid as monthly income. Larger investors earn 1.2–2 per cent more than smaller investors.

**Tax** Interest is paid net of tax; higher rate taxpayers pay more. Gross interest is available for registered non-taxpayers.

**Children** Yes. Particularly for their long-term savings. Parent's signature is required for under-sevens.

**How to invest** Most societies have notice accounts. Apply at a branch. Postal service is frequently available.

**Record** Passbook.

**Money Mail Rating** *****

**Investor protection** Building society savings compensation scheme covers 90 per cent of savings up to £20,000. Maximum payout £18,000 per person.

**Comment** Rates vary widely between societies and you can get up to 2 per cent more before tax by choosing the right society. Coventry and Yorkshire are often among the best payers on 90 day accounts. Check the compound annual rate if interest is paid monthly. When interest rates are fluctuating, give your relevant notice immediately you make an investment in order to be able to switch funds quickly if a better interest rate opportunity appears.

# Ordinary or Share Account

The basic no-strings, no-extras building society account offering easy access and miserly interest rates should be avoided. Opt for an instant access account with a low minimum balance instead. A deposit account, in return for 100 per cent security, has slightly lower interest rate.

| | |
|---|---|
| Suitable for | It is hard to make a case for anyone. These accounts are very much the poor relation in the range. |
| Open to | Anyone. |
| Min–Max | £1. No maximum. |
| Charges | None generally, but Halifax has introduced a transaction charge for small savers. |
| Withdrawals | On demand from any branch or agency up to £250 in cash; by cheque from branches up to £5,000. |
| Interest | Variable; paid half-yearly to be accumulated or paid by cheque or direct into a bank or other building society account. |
| Tax | Interest is paid net of tax; higher rate taxpayers pay more. Building societies can pay interest gross to non-taxpayers; non-taxpayers who fail to register will still be able to reclaim the basic rate of tax deducted at source. |
| Children | Yes, but parent's signature is required for under-sevens. |
| How to invest | At a local branch or agency. |
| Record | Passbook. |
| Money Mail Rating | ***** |
| Investor protection | Building society compensation scheme covers 90 per cent of savings up to £20,000. Maximum payout £18,000 per person. |

**Comment** Increasingly obsolete account. Use Nationwide's Cashbuilder account, an instant access account with minimum opening balance of £1. Once you reach £100–£250 the choice gets wider with Leeds & Holbeck and National & Provincial. Children's Accounts frequently pay more to young savers irrespective of balance. Deposit accounts should be ignored.

# Postal Account

A growing number of building societies operate accounts which are run exclusively through the post rather than the branch network. They offer attractive interest rates for those willing to operate the account using the first class post rather than a local branch. You can usually get your money back on demand but allow a couple of days for the post.

**Suitable for** Anyone looking for good returns who is happy to run their account outside the High Street.

**Open to** Anyone.

**Min–Max** £1,000–£2,500; no maximum.

**Charges** None.

**Withdrawals** At any time on instructions sent via the post. The society provides paying-in and withdrawal slips.

**Interest** Variable and tiered so that the more you have in your account, the more you earn. Interest is usually paid annually or monthly.

**Tax** Interest is paid net of tax; higher rate taxpayers pay more. Building societies can pay interest gross to non-taxpayers; non-taxpayers who fail to register will still be able to reclaim the basic rate of tax deducted at source.

**Children** Yes, parents operate the account.

**How to invest** Through the post. Cheltenham & Gloucester allow you to open an account through their branch network, but thereafter it must be run through the post. Societies offering good postal accounts include Birmingham Midshires, Bradford & Bingley, Chelsea (with cheque book), Cheltenham & Gloucester, Britannia and Northern Rock. Other societies to watch which sometimes offer good accounts include Leeds & Holbeck, Norwich & Peterborough, Nottingham and Scarborough. Bristol and West now operate a telephone dealing service. You can also operate Cheltenham & Gloucester and Bradford & Bingley accounts by telephone.

**Record** Regular statements.

**Money Mail Rating** *****

**Investor protection** Building society compensation scheme covers 90 per cent of savings up to £20,000. Maximum payout £18,000 per person.

**Comment** Cheltenham & Gloucester has traditionally paid good rates on its account, and Bradford & Bingley is determined to follow in its footsteps. Both accounts pay attractive annual and monthly rates: Bradford & Bingley's rate is tiered, starting at £1,000, while Cheltenham & Gloucester starts at £2,500 or £5,000 for monthly income.

# Regular Savings Account

Regular monthly savings scheme for unlimited period paying investors a higher rate of interest than on an ordinary account. One withdrawal a year is sometimes allowed, so is one month's savings lapse. It is usually possible to vary the amount saved.

**Suitable for** Short-to-medium savings goals, such as a holiday, and more particularly a house.

**Open to** Anyone.

**Min–Max** £1–£10 a month minimum; £100–£250 maximum (doubled for joint accounts).

**Charges** None.

**Withdrawals** Partial withdrawals once or twice a year may be permitted, otherwise the account is closed or transferred to an ordinary account.

**Interest** Variable, paid half-yearly or annually and usually accumulated in the account. The rate is 1–1½ per cent above the ordinary rate.

**Tax** Interest is paid net of tax; higher rate taxpayers pay more. Building societies can pay interest gross to non-taxpayers; non-taxpayers who fail to register will still be able to reclaim the basic rate of tax deducted at source.

**Children** Not suitable.

**How to invest** Most societies offer a regular savings scheme; apply at a branch.

**Record** Passbook.

**Money Mail Rating** *****

**Investor protection** Building society savings compensation scheme covers 90 per cent of savings up to £20,000. Maximum payout £18,000 per person.

**Comment** Interest rates on these accounts are not at the top of the building society range, so savers should use the account as a stepping stone to building up sufficient capital to transfer to a higher-paying instant access account.

# Save As You Earn (SAYE)

2nd Issue

Regular monthly savings scheme for five years with option to leave investment for further two. Interest, which accumulates, is tax free and there is a bonus equivalent to 14 months' payments, tax free, at the end of five years, or 28 months' if you leave the savings in for the next two years. A gap of six months' savings can be made up.

**Suitable for** Higher rate taxpayers; regular savings for an unspecified purpose, particularly when interest rates are falling.

**Open to** Anyone aged 16 or over.

**Min–Max** £1 a month; £20 maximum.

**Charges** None.

**Withdrawals** No partial withdrawals; repayment takes two to three weeks. Reduced interest rate penalties on early withdrawals: no interest in year one, years two to five interest of 6 per cent only (8 per cent if you die).

**Interest** Fixed. Including the bonus, the rate is equivalent to 8.3 per cent a year over five years; including the enlarged bonus, the rate over seven years is equivalent to 8.62 per cent a year. It accumulates and is paid out when the contract matures.

**Tax** Tax free.

**Children** No.

**How to invest** Many societies operate a SAYE account; apply at a branch.

**Record** Certificate.

**Money Mail Rating** *****

**Investor protection** Building society savings compensation scheme covers 90 per cent of savings up to £20,000.

**Comment** Be sure you can keep up the savings for five years; early surrender rates are unattractive.

# Save As You Earn (SAYE)

Series "F" Share Option Scheme

Regular monthly savings linked to a company share option scheme. Employees are offered the option to buy shares at a price fixed at the start of the five-year savings period which cannot be less than 80 per cent of market value. Employees invest a set amount each month in the SAYE scheme. At the end of five years they can either use the money to exercise the share option or take the money with a bonus; they can leave the money invested for another two years to obtain a higher bonus BUT they will then lose the share option entitlement. However, some employers offer a seven-year share option plan when the share option can then be exercised.

Interest in the SAYE accumulates tax free. In addition there is a bonus of 9 months' payments tax free at the end of five years, or 18 months' if you leave the savings in for the next two years.

**Suitable for** Employees who want to build up a share stake in their company.

**Open to** Employers running a scheme fix the eligibility rules, usually determined by length of service with the company. Employees may have more than one share option SAYE scheme, provided the overall monthly contribution does not exceed the maximum.

**Min–Max** £10 a month minimum; £250 a month maximum.

**Charges** None.

**Withdrawals** No partial withdrawals. Reduced interest rate penalties on early withdrawal; no interest in year one; years two to five, 5 per cent. If you die, your executor can either take the amount saved or buy shares at the option price.

**Interest** Fixed. Including the bonus, interest is equivalent to 5.3 per cent over five years; including the enlarged bonus, the rate over seven years is equivalent to 5.87 per cent. It is accumulated.

**Tax** Tax free. Once the share option is exercised, dividends are taxable and there is a potential gains tax liability, based on the actual purchase price of the shares, when you sell them.

**Children** No.

**How to invest** You will be invited to participate by your employer who must have Inland Revenue approval for the scheme.

**Record** Certificate.

**Money Mail Rating** ***** until the share option is exercised.

**Investor protection** Building societies compensation scheme covers 90 per cent of savings up to £20,000. Maximum payout £18,000 per person.

**Comment** A useful way of hedging your bets. If the company's shares have risen since you were granted the option, then you exercise the option and buy the share at the lower price fixed when you began saving. You will have a built-in profit. However, if your company has been less successful and the share price is actually lower than the option price, then take the SAYE proceeds as cash.

# Tax Exempt Special Savings Account

Tessa, for short, is a new form of saving introduced at the beginning of 1991. It is a five year account for either regular or irregular lump sum savings and provided the capital is left intact for five years, the interest is tax free. If the interest is withdrawn before then, it will be paid net of basic rate tax, but the amount reserved for tax will be paid as a tax-free bonus at the end of the five year period. If the capital is withdrawn before, the interest is taxable.

**Suitable for** Erratic lump sum savers, taxpayers and "rainy day" savings.

**Open to** Anyone over 18.

**Min–Max** Overall maximum over five years, £9,000. Maximum per month £150. Maximum lump sum £3,000 in year one, £1,800 in years two to four, £600 in year five.

**Charges** None.

**Withdrawals** Interest can be taken net within the five year period. Capital can be taken at any time, but tax advantages will be lost.

**Interest** Variable, usually annually.

**Tax** Interest is tax free provided capital is not withdrawn early. If net interest is taken during the five year span, the amount reserved for tax will be paid as a tax-free bonus at the end of the term.

**Children** No.

**Record** Initial certificate and annual update.

**Money Mail Rating** *****

**Comment** An attractive and flexible savings vehicle, suitable for second level emergency savings. Tessas may be transferred from one financial institution to another but this may entail a loss of bonus or a charge. Not all providers allow transfers into their scheme. Pick a plan with attractive rates and no transfer penalties. Alliance & Leicester and Yorkshire are two large societies which have, to date, offered consistently competitive rates. Compare with plans on offer from banks and other deposit takers.

# Term Share

Lump sum investment of renewed popularity. Investors' funds are locked in for a period – the term – of one to five years, although withdrawals are sometimes permitted with a loss of interest penalty. Interest rates are at the high end of the building society range, and often include a guaranteed differential over ordinary rate. In a period of low interest rates, building societies are anxious to tie in savers with term shares. In response to the new (1994) National Savings Pensioners Guaranteed Income Bond interest rates are becoming more attractive.

| | |
|---|---|
| Suitable for | Modest lump sums which are too low to trigger off the top rates available on other accounts, provided the money is not going to be required. |
| Open to | Anyone. |
| Min–Max | £500–£1,000 minimum; no maximum. |
| Charges | None. |
| Withdrawals | Usually not allowed. Capital plus interest earned to date is repaid on death within the term.. |
| Interest | Usually variable, paid annually, half-yearly or monthly. |
| Tax | Interest is paid net of tax; higher rate taxpayers must pay more. Building societies can pay interest gross to non-taxpayers; non-taxpayers who fail to register will still be able to reclaim the basic rate of tax deducted at source. |
| Children | As tax paid, suitable for parents' gift of money. Parents who pay the higher rate of tax will have to pay more. National Savings Certificates and Children's Bonus Bonds are generally a better buy. |
| How to invest | Mainly offered by medium and smaller societies, and not always available. Apply at branches or by post or through newspaper advertisements. |
| Record | Passbook or certificate. |

**Money Mail Rating** *****

**Investor protection** Building society savings compensation scheme covers 90 per cent of savings up to £20,000. Maximum payout £18,000 per person.

**Comment** An inflexible form of savings, and longer-term periods should be avoided. Always check the withdrawal options. Investors with larger sums will be able to obtain a higher interest on a more flexible instant access or notice account. Fixed interest term shares can be attractive when interest rates are falling, however. The guaranteed differential above the ordinary share rate can be less generous than it sounds, as ordinary share rates tend to rise more slowly and fall further than other account rates.

CHAPTER 12

# Gold

## Gold Coins

Gold coins are the easiest and most reliable way for a private investor to take a direct stake in gold. As a coin it is a non-income producing asset, it is held either purely for speculation that the price of gold, which can fluctuate considerably, will rise; or for the simple pleasure of owning it. The modern coins contain one Troy ounce of gold but stand at a premium to the price of gold, quoted in dollars per ounce. The EC banned the importation of South African Krugerrands in 1986. Other popular coins include the Canadian Maple Leaf and the Chinese Panda. The UK began minting a new gold coin, the Britannia, in 1987.

**Suitable for** At the most 5 per cent to 10 per cent of savings and then only out of capital which will not be required at short notice. Alternative to cash gifts.

**Open to** Anyone.

**Min–Max** Current price of one gold coin – £261–£263, February 1994; – or less for Sovereigns which contain 0.2354 Troy oz gold – £60–£63, February 1994. No maximum.

**Charges** Commission included in price of coin; 17.5 per cent VAT charged on all coins bought in the UK (except those more than 100 years old, where VAT is charged on the dealer's profit margins only). Coins bought and held in the Channel Islands or Gibraltar are not subject to VAT, but attract a storage charge of typically £2 a coin and an annual service fee of 50p per half-year, paid in arrears.

**Withdrawals** At current market price, immediately.

**Tax** Capital gains tax liability on profits except for pre-1838 Sovereigns.

**Children** Gifts.

**How to invest** Check prices, quoted in dollars, in newspaper. Most banks buy and sell gold coins but usually impose a minimum of 10 coins/£3,000. Compare prices charged by dealers. A full coin dealing (and storage if required) service is available from Braid & Co, Gold Investments Ltd and Spink & Son Ltd. If you deal through the Channel Islands and keep the coins there to avoid VAT, stick to subsidiaries of well-known UK banks.

**Record** If you hold the coins yourself, none. If coins are held offshore, certificate and regular statement.

**Money Mail Rating** *!!!! to !!!!!

**Investor protection** Gold coins fall outside the scope of the Financial Services Act; in the UK store coins at bank; if coins are kept in the Channel Islands, make sure the coins are physically held in your name.

**Comment** A limited exposure to gold can be very rewarding, particularly at times of international political uncertainty or strong currency fluctuations. However, it is worth noting that the gold price did not surge ahead in the Gulf War, as might have been expected. A platinum coin, the Isle of Man Noble, is also available, and in several denominations.

CHAPTER 13

# Friendly Society

## Regular Savings Policy

A regular savings scheme, with contributions paid monthly, half yearly or annually, for a 10-year period. It is a form of life assurance contract invested in a tax-free investment fund; at least half the premium income is to be invested in fixed interest investments such as Government securities or building societies. The remainder is often invested in unit trusts.

| | |
|---|---|
| Suitable for | Regular savings for yourself or for a child which you are sure you can maintain; higher rate taxpayers. |
| Open to | Anyone aged 18 or over. |
| Min–Max | A minimum of £9 a month or £60 to £100 a year. A maximum of £18 a month or £200 a year. Each person is only permitted one policy in all. Married couples each take one out. (A policy taken out before 13 March 1984 could have a higher premium.) |
| Charges | Built into your premium. |
| Withdrawals | If you withdraw your funds before the end of the 10-year term then you will receive a return of contributions only. After 10 years the policy pro- |

ceeds can be withdrawn or left to earn interest. On death within 10 years guaranteed life cover of £750 to £1,000 is paid out.

**Interest** Variable. It is reinvested.

**Tax** Proceeds are free of income and capital gains tax.

**Children** Investment can be made on behalf of a child with a maximum of one policy per child.

**How to invest** Obtain application forms from a friendly society such as Family, Fleet, Homeowners, Manchester Unity, Time Assurance and Tunbridge Wells.

**Record** Insurance Policy.

**Money Mail Rating** ****!

**Comment** There is no point in taking out such a contract unless it stays in force for 10 years; building society linked schemes offer better value. Plans linked to unit trusts are inflexible compared with regular savings into units via either a unit trust regular savings (effectively free of capital gains tax) scheme or a personal equity plan (free of capital gains tax). Larger premium policies are partly invested in conventional life assurance funds which do not roll up tax-free.

CHAPTER 14

# Life Insurance

## Annuity

A lump sum investment which cannot be redeemed, in return for which investors receive an income for life. The amount payable will depend upon your age: the older you are, the better the return. The interest paid is usually fixed at the outset. Annuity contracts can be varied to provide an income which continues until the surviving spouse dies, or a guaranteed income which continues for five or 10 years regardless of whether the annuitant survives.

**Suitable for** Older men and women; fixed income offers little protection against rising costs in periods of high inflation.

**Open to** Anyone, in theory, but rarely worthwhile for people under 70 (men) or 75 (women).

**Min–Max** Minimum realistic level is around £1,000 – producing (at February 1994) around £117 p.a. income for men aged 70 and £123 for women aged 75. No maximum.

**Charges** Built into the contract terms.

**Withdrawals** None.

**Interest** Fixed, according to each type of annuity. A few unit-linked contracts provide rising interest from a much lower starting base. Interest is usually paid in arrears by cheque or direct to a bank account monthly, quarterly, half-yearly or annually.

**Tax** Part of the annuity is treated as return of capital and is tax free, the remainder is treated as income and has basic rate tax deducted at source. Non-taxpayers can be paid gross; higher rate taxpayers pay more.

**Children** Not suitable.

**How to invest** Most life insurance companies offer annuities. Check rates in specialist publications such as *Money Management* or *Planned Savings* and/or consult an insurance broker.

**Record** Annuity contract, setting out the terms.

**Money Mail Rating** *****

**Investor protection** Policyholders' protection scheme covers 90 per cent of benefits.

**Comment** With modest inflation only, annuities can be worthwhile for the more elderly. They can also be useful for inheritance tax planning for people with large estates. Older men and women owning their own property can release some of the capital "tied up" in the house with the use of Income Plan, based upon an annuity and mortgage package.

# Distribution Bond

This is an important subset of the Investment Bond category. It is a lump sum investment into a mainstream single premium life insurance policy which is the standard mix of gilt-edged securities, shares both in the UK and overseas, and property. The main difference between it and a conventional investment bond is that instead of rolling the income up in the life fund, the managers distribute it to investors, usually half-yearly. In addition it is possible to top up the income from capital.

**Suitable for** Higher rate taxpayers and older people who need to augment their retirement income, particularly those who near the ceiling for age allowance, the extra tax allowance given to those on modest income aged 65 years or more.

**Open to** It varies from company to company, but age 14 to 80 are common limits.

**Min–Max** Varies. Ranges from £2,500 to £100,000, but £5,000 to £50,000 are more typical limits.

**Charges** An initial fee, commonly of 5 per cent, is deducted from the initial investment; there is also an annual fee of 1–1.5 per cent.

**Interest** Variable; most managers aim to provide rising income; it is possible to use a tax-efficient "withdrawal" facility which enables investors to withdraw a certain amount of capital to top up income. Provided no more than 5 per cent is withdrawn, it is tax free to basic rate taxpayers while higher rate taxpayers can defer their tax liability (on the difference between the 25 per cent basic rate and 40 per cent higher rate band) for twenty years. The assumption is that by that time, many bondholders will have retired and no longer be 40 per cent rate taxpayers, and therefore will not have to pay any tax after all.

**Tax** Income tax and capital gains tax on realised gains are paid by the insurance company and are thus reflected in the underlying unit price. The proceeds are tax free for basic rate taxpayers; non-taxpayers cannot reclaim any income tax paid; higher rate taxpayers must pay more.

**Children** Yes, if age limits permit.

**How to invest** Buy direct from an insurance company; use the services of an independent financial adviser to find the one most suitable for your needs.

**Record** Insurance policy.

**Money Mail Rating** **!!! to ****!

**Investor protection** Policyholders' Protection Act covers 90 per cent of your savings.

**Comment** These are conservatively managed investments, with a record of rising income (from investments rather than capital withdrawal). However, the bond is more heavily taxed internally than unit and investment trusts. They are likely to show a steady rather than volatile investment performance.

# Guaranteed Income Bond and Guaranteed Growth Bond

A lump sum investment with a fixed return over a term of one to five years (commonly), sometimes six to 10 years and, rarely, as long as 15 years. If the bond pays out the interest, it is an Income Bond; if the income is accumulated, it is a Growth Bond. Underlying investments linked to fixed rate investments.

**Suitable for** Augmenting retirement income (but check the age allowance, see page **31**); building up capital before retirement; specific savings target (Growth Bonds); taking a view on interest rates.

**Open to** Minimum age is often 16 or 18; maximum age is commonly 80 or 85, occasionally 90.

**Min–Max** Minimum £1,000–£2,000. Maximum none, or £50,000, £75,000 or £100,000.

**Charges** Built into contract terms.

**Withdrawals** At maturity, original investment – Income Bonds; guaranteed value – Growth Bonds; early surrender values, if available, are usually poor. Death benefits: original investment – Income Bonds; original investment plus 6–9 per cent – Growth Bonds.

**Interest** Fixed. Income Bonds pay monthly (the rate is usually marginally lower), half-yearly and most commonly annually. Interest accumulates with Growth Bonds.

**Tax** Interest is paid net of tax (Growth and Income Bonds alike) which usually cannot be reclaimed by non-taxpayers; higher rate taxpayers pay more.

**Children** Not suitable.

**How to invest** Some bonds are only available for a limited period – check newspapers for offers. Check rates in specialist publications such as *Money Management* or *Planned Savings* and/or consult an insurance broker. Stick to UK insurance companies.

**Record** Insurance policy.

**Money Mail Rating** *****

**Investor protection** Policyholders' protection scheme covers 90 per cent of benefits agreed by UK insurance companies, provided they are not excessive.

**Comment** High fixed returns are attractive if you think interest rates will fall. Insurance companies carefully "match" their underlying investments to provide the guaranteed return at a set date; but the guarantee is still only as good as the company issuing it, so always choose an authorised UK insurance company. Policies sold by an overseas life insurance company which is not authorised in the UK are not included in the policyholders' protection scheme.

# Guaranteed Stock Market Bond

This the most novel form of investment bond yet. The basic Investment Bond (see page 81) is a lump sum investment into a single premium insurance policy linked to the stock market. The Guaranteed Stock Market Bond goes one stage further by letting you benefit from the gains on the stock market at the same time as shielding you from potential losses. Companies offering these bonds in effect insure against the risk of falling markets by using sophisticated investment tools known as "derivatives" or futures and options.

But the cost of protecting investors against a stock market fall has to be paid for. This normally means giving up the income from your investment. A bond will normally promise to match some or all of the capital growth of the market, even if subsequently it were to fall, but in return you sacrifice any income the bond might have earned. Guaranteed Stock Market Bonds sound a lot more complicated than they actually are.

| | |
|---|---|
| Suitable for | Cautious investors. Once your investment has achieved a certain level, that gain will be locked in and cannot be taken away. It is conceivable that you might not make money if the stock market were to go into decline, but nor would you lose it either. |
| Open to | Varies according to company; 14 to 80 years of age are the most extreme limits. |
| Min–Max | Varies. £1,000 is a common minimum. |
| Charges | Initial fees of around 5 per cent and an annual fee of 1–1.5 per cent. |
| Interest | None. |
| Tax | The insurance company pays income tax and capital gains tax on realised gains, which is reflected in the underlying unit price. The proceeds are tax free for basic rate taxpayers; higher rate taxpayers must pay more. |
| Children | Yes, if age limits permit. |
| How to invest | Direct from a company (these bonds are heavily advertised in the press), or use the services of an independent financial adviser for a recommendation from a selection of bonds. |
| Record | A policy which looks like an investment certificate. |
| Money Mail Rating | ****! |

**Investor Protection** Policyholders' Protection Act covers 90 per cent of the unit value.

**Comment** The bonds are a half-way house between depositing your money and earning interest and having a go on the stock market. But you are reliant entirely on capital growth for your return, as income has been sacrificed for the guarantee against losses.

# Investment Bond

A lump sum investment in the form of a single-premium life insurance policy linked directly to an individual market sector, or mixture of different types of investment. There are investment bonds linked to UK equities, international equities, fixed interest stock, cash, convertible stock and property (Property Bond), both in the UK or overseas. Other bonds, known as Managed Bonds, are linked to a mixture of some or all of these investment categories. Investors can switch to one category from another in the same group without cashing in the policy.

**Suitable for** Higher rate taxpayers and older people on modest incomes who are borderline cases in respect of the age allowance (see page **31**), the extra tax relief given to some people over the age of 65.

**Open to** Varies; anyone, usually from 14 to 80 years of age.

**Min–Max** £500, commonly £1,000 and sometimes £2,500 minimum. No maximum.

**Charges** An initial fee of 3–10 per cent is deducted from the initial investment; annual fee of ½–¾ per cent.

**Withdrawals** On demand, at current market value; on death current market value of units (more in earlier years).

**Interest** Variable; accumulated within the fund. Up to 5 per cent of original investment can be withdrawn as "income" with income tax liability (applicable to higher rate taxpayers only) deferred until the bond is finally encashed, or after 20 years. "Income" withdrawal does not have to be declared on your tax return.

**Tax** Income tax and capital gains tax apply to realised gains paid by the insurance company, reflected in the underlying unit price. The proceeds are tax free for basic rate taxpayers; non-taxpayers cannot reclaim any income tax paid; higher rate taxpayers must pay more.

**Children** Yes, where age limits permit.

**How to invest** Check the performance of underlying units in specialist publications such as *Money Management* or *Planned Savings*; phone or write for details from insurance companies before investing.

**Record** Insurance policy.

**Money Mail Rating** ****! to *!!!!

**Investor protection** Policyholders' protection scheme covers 90 per cent of current unit value.

**Comment** This bond's internal capital gains tax liability is a major disadvantage compared with lump sum investment in unit trusts which roll up without capital gains tax. "Income" withdrawal is beneficial to higher rate taxpayers who can defer tax liability until retirement when their tax bracket is likely to be lower; older people will not have their age allowance entitlement jeopardised by "income" withdrawal.

# School Fees Educational Trust

A lump sum investment via a trust into a life insurance company for a child which will pay school fees on either a flat or increasing basis. It can be taken out immediately before the fees become due, or up to 13 years in advance. It is not essential to identify the school in advance, and you can change your mind and surrender the policy instead. Regular savings are sometimes permitted if the policy is taken out at least three years ahead of first fee.

**Suitable for** Parents, grandparents and any adult wishing to fund school fees in advance, particularly higher rate taxpayers.

| | |
|---|---|
| Open to | Anyone. |
| Min–Max | Depends on the size of fees and the number of years ahead they are required. Minimum £500–£2,500; £50 a month; no maximum. |
| Charges | Built into the contract. |
| Withdrawals | Paid as agreed termly fees; if the child dies, 95–100 per cent of the original purchase price plus interest is returned; otherwise non-guaranteed surrender value. |
| Interest | Fixed; accumulated within the trust. |
| Tax | The fees from the trust are paid tax free as the person making the payment has no legal interest in the policy. |
| Children | Improbable – the trust is for their benefit. |
| How to invest | Equitable Life (which accepts monthly and irregular lump sum contributions), Royal Life, Save & Prosper, and School Fees Insurance Agency (SFIA) all have educational trust facilities. |
| Record | Contract with trust. |
| Money Mail Rating | ***** |
| Investor protection | Policyholders' protection scheme covers 90 per cent of benefits. |
| Comment | More flexible than investing school fees in advance via a "composition fee" scheme direct with the school of your choice. The earlier the school fee investment is made, the smaller the capital outlay. |

# Unit-Linked Regular Savings Plan

A regular savings insurance policy for five or 10 years or indefinitely, linked directly to an individual market sector, or to a mixture of different types of investment. Savings can be linked to specific unit trusts, UK equities, international equities, fixed interest stock, cash, property or a mixture of some or all of these categories. Investors can switch their savings from one category to another.

**Suitable for** One-stop financial planning, as policies can be adapted to provide more protection and less investment content, and vice-versa at different intervals, such as marriage or the birth of children; insurance backing to a mortgage instead of a conventional endowment policy.

**Open to** Varies; anyone from 13 to 70 years old.

**Min–Max** £10–£50 minimum; no maximum.

**Charges** Policy fee – from none to £1.30 per month; the initial fee of 4–5 per cent is deducted from the premium; annual fee ¾–1 per cent.

**Withdrawals** After 10 years you get the value of the units; before that there might be a capital gains tax liability. There is usually surrender penalty if the policy encashed in early years.

**Interest** Variable; accumulated within the fund.

**Tax** Income tax and capital gains tax on both the realised and unrealised gains paid by the insurance company, reflected in the underlying unit price. Proceeds are tax free after 10 years; on earlier encashment, higher rate taxpayers pay more.

**Children** Yes, where age limits permit.

**How to invest** Check the performance of underlying units in specialist publications such as *Money Management* or *Planned Savings*; most companies offer this contract, so phone or write for details. Independent intermediaries will be able to advise on these schemes.

**Record** Insurance policy and annual unit valuation.

**Money Mail Rating** ****! to *!!!!

**Investor protection** Policyholders' protection scheme covers 90 per cent of current unit value.

**Comment** The capital gains tax liability on underlying investments is a major disadvantage compared with regular savings directly into unit trusts which roll up free of capital gains tax. As the proceeds are tax free, however, there can be tax planning opportunities. These unit-linked plans are becoming increasingly popular as an alternative to endowment policies for backing an interest-only mortgage. If the underlying units rise rapidly, the home loan can be repaid earlier.

## With-Profits Endowment Policy

A regular savings policy for a fixed period of 10 years or more. A guaranteed sum assured is paid out on death before the end of the set term or at maturity *plus* any bonuses which the policy has earned from the underlying investments. There are two kinds of bonuses: those declared annually ("reversionary bonuses", which can never be taken away from the policy), and a "terminal bonus", which can vary, paid out at maturity.

**Suitable for** Nowadays used mainly in connection with house purchase, particularly the "low cost" endowment variation; regular savings which are not required for several years.

**Open to** Anyone from eight years old.

**Charges** Built into the contract; policy fee of around £1 a month.

**Min–Max** £5–£10 a month minimum; no maximum.

**Withdrawals** On maturity or the death beforehand of the life assured (usually the policyholder's, but it can be another person in whom you have an "insurable", in other words financial, interest). Surrender values are non-existent or very low in the first few years, and the surrender penalty remains heavy for several or many years afterwards.

Alternatively, the policyholder can stop paying premiums and make the policy "paid up" at a reduced benefit level. It is also possible to take out a loan against the policy from the insurance company, often at competitive rates.

**Interest** Variable; built into bonuses.

**Tax** Income tax and capital gains tax on realised profits paid by the insurance company, reflected in the level of bonuses. Policy proceeds after 10 years are completely tax free, but on earlier encashment higher rate taxpayers can pay more.

**Children** Policies "in trust" for a child avoid inheritance tax; children over eight years can take out a policy, but a parent's signature is required up to 18.

**How to invest** Consult an insurance broker or obtain quotes direct from life offices and compare. Equitable Life, which does not pay commission, will not be included on broker quotations.

**Record** Insurance policy; annual bonus statement.

**Money Mail Rating** ****!

**Investor protection** Policyholders' protection scheme covers 90 per cent of benefits.

**Comment** Long-term endowment policies with harsh surrender policies should be avoided. This is an inflexible and increasingly outmoded form of savings, largely used now in connection with house purchase. Terminal bonus rates have begun to be lower in the last two years.

# With-Profits Flexible Policy

A regular savings policy for an indefinite period, which should be for at least 10 years. On death a guaranteed sum assured is paid out plus any bonuses which the policy has earned from its underlying investments. After 10 years the policy can be encashed at any time without a surrender penalty at a guaranteed or part-guaranteed value. The policy is often issued as a cluster of small identical policies which can each be cashed in separately.

**Suitable for** Regular savings, particularly for specific targets, such as school fees, needed at least 10 years hence.

**Open to** Anyone from eight years.

**Min–Max** £10–£25 a month minimum; no maximum.

**Charges** Built into the contract; policy fee of around £1 a month.

**Withdrawals** On the death of the life assured, when a guaranteed sum assured plus bonuses is paid; at guaranteed surrender value any time after 10 years. Harsh surrender penalties apply to withdrawals before 10 years.

**Interest** Variable; built into bonuses.

**Tax** Income tax and capital gains tax on the realised profits paid by the insurance company, reflected in the level of bonuses. Policy proceeds after 10 years are completely tax free, but on earlier encashment higher rate taxpayers can pay more.

**Children** Policies "in trust" for a child avoid inheritance tax; children over eight years can take out a policy, but a parent's signature required up to 18.

**How to invest** Consult an insurance broker or obtain quotes direct from life offices and compare.

**Record** Insurance policy; annual bonus statement.

**Money Mail Rating** ****!

**Investor protection** Policyholders' protection scheme covers 90 per cent of benefits.

**Comment** More flexible than a with-profit endowment policy which it was partially designed to replace. Cluster policies, where each bit can be cashed separately, give more flexibility still. At maturity proceeds can be left intact and a nominal premium, around £5 p.a., allows the policyholder to withdraw regular tax-free "income" from the policy, or take out tax-free money at irregular intervals.

## With-Profit Bonds

Broadly the same as a with-profits endowment policy but for a lump sum investment rather than regular savings. Effectively an investment in the equity and property markets, usually with an element of gilts and cash, but the fluctuations are smoothed out by the insurance companies who use their reserves to bolster the return in poor years, replenishing those reserves in good years. The bond earns a return through two types of bonus: those declared annually ("reversionary bonuses", which can never be taken away from the policy), and a "terminal bonus", which can vary, paid out at maturity.

**Suitable for** Investors who want to "strip out" an income and for those who want to benefit from stockmarket/property growth without the usual fluctuations.

**Open to** Anyone.

**Charges** Built into the contract.

| | |
|---|---|
| Min–Max | £1,000–£5,000; no maximum. |
| Withdrawals | On demand at current market value, but the company can use a market value adjuster to reduce the value if market conditions are exceptionally poor. On death at current market value of units. |
| Charges | Initial fee usually of around 5 per cent but can be reduced for larger investments. An annual fee is built into the contract. |
| Interest | None, but withdrawals can be made on a regular basis by selling units monthly, quarterly, half-yearly or annually. This can provide an income at whatever level the investor chooses. |
| Tax | Income tax and capital gains tax on realised profits paid by insurance company, reflected in level of bonuses. Policy proceeds are tax free but higher rate taxpayers can pay more. |
| Children | Policies "in trust" for a child avoid inheritance tax if held for seven years and could mitigate inheritance tax if held for shorter periods. Children over eight can invest but a parent's signature is required until 18. |
| How to invest | Consult a financial adviser or obtain quotes direct from life offices and compare. Look for companies with a good record of bonus payments and good reserves. |
| Record | Insurance policy; annual bonus statement. |
| Money Mail Rating | ****! |
| Investor protection | Policyholders' protection scheme covers 90 per cent of benefits. |
| Comment | Can buy/sell on any business day but should be regarded as a long-term investment if stripping out an income. |

# Temporary Annuity and "Back to Backs"

A temporary annuity is a lump sum investment which cannot be redeemed, in return for a high income for a specified period, usually five or 10 years. There is no return of capital at maturity so it is common to link the temporary annuity with a growth vehicle – usually an investment bond, unit trust or PEP – which is designed to return the original capital. This is called a "back-to-back" arrangement. A £10,000 investment can, for example, be split into a £4,000 temporary annuity to provide a high income over five years and a £6,000 PEP investment which it is hoped will grow to £10,000 over the five years.

**Suitable for** Anyone looking for a high regular income who is prepared to accept the moderate degree of risk.

**Open to** Anyone.

**Min–Max** Usually £5,000; no maximum.

**Charges** Built into the contract. See appropriate sections for growth vehicles.

**Interest** Fixed. Usually paid in arrears by cheque or direct to a bank account monthly, quarterly, half-yearly or annually.

**Tax** Part of the annuity is treated as a return of capital and is tax free, the remainder is treated as income and is paid net of basic rate tax. Non-taxpayers can be paid gross; higher rate taxpayers pay more. See appropriate sections for growth vehicles.

**Children** Possible but not particularly suitable.

**How to invest** Look for advertisements in the financial press and check performances of growth vehicles in specialist publications such as *Money Management* or *Planned Savings*; phone or write to the relevant companies to ask for details before investing.

**Record** Annuity contract.

**Money Mail Rating** *****

**Investor protection** Policyholders' protection scheme covers 90 per cent of annuity benefits.

**Comment** Usually a way of providing a better income than a building society, but much depends on the performance of the growth vehicle. It could provide a return equal to or more than the original capital but there is a risk that it could provide less. See comment in appropriate sections for each type of growth vehicle.

CHAPTER 15

# Local Authorities

## Fixed Term Loan

A lump sum investment paying a fixed rate of interest for a set period of one to 10 years. Shorter term loans are available for larger sums.

**Suitable for** Lock-away savings only or savings with a specific target date; five years is generally long enough to commit yourself to one form of savings. Non-taxpayers should consider Government stock on the National Savings Stock Register.

**Open to** Anyone aged 18 or over.

**Min–Max** Varies. Minimum can be as little as £100–£500, although £1,000 is more common.

**Charges** None.

**Withdrawals** Not permitted until end of term.

**Interest** Fixed; usually paid half-yearly.

**Tax** Interest paid net of tax; higher rate taxpayers pay extra. Local authorities can pay interest gross to non-taxpayers.

**Children** An investment can be made on behalf of a child, but this is not really suitable.

**How to invest** Newspaper coupons, or direct from a local authority (treasurer's department).

**Record** Certificate.

**Money Mail Rating** *****

**Comment** When interest rates are falling, fixed rate returns can be attractive (conversely if they are rising). The main drawback is the inflexibility. The fixed term means precisely what it says: most local authority treasurers will not permit early repayment, no matter the hardship: death is the only exception. Investors with more than £25,000 might be able to negotiate better rates.

# Negotiable or Yearling Bond

A lump sum investment paying a fixed rate of interest for a set period, normally one year, hence the name "yearling". Local authorities parcel up a selection of loan requirements into a single bond which can be bought and sold on the Stock Exchange. Investors don't identify the specific authorities behind the issue but treat it like any other fixed interest, negotiable security, such as Government stock. The bonds might be issued at a very small discount to the nominal value.

**Suitable for** Any short-term fixed interest investment where flexibility is required.

**Open to** Anyone aged 18 or over.

**Min–Max** Buy in multiples of £1,000, the minimum investment is £1,000. No maximum.

**Charges** None, if bought as a new issue from a stockbroker and held to redemption; otherwise stockbroker's commission if you buy and sell between those dates.

**Withdrawals** Hold to maturity for return of full nominal value or sell before on the Stock Exchange where the price can vary.

**Interest** Fixed, paid half-yearly; any interest due is added to the selling price if you sell the bonds early.

**Tax** Basic rate tax is deducted at source but can be reclaimed by non-taxpayers; higher rate taxpayers pay extra. If you sell at a profit the gain is liable to capital gains tax.

**Children** Investment can be made on behalf of a child, but is not suitable.

**How to invest** Through a stockbroker or bank share dealing service.

**Record** Certificate.

**Money Mail Rating** If held to maturity *****. If sold early ****!

**Comment** Flexible: if there is any upward movement in interest rates you are not locked in; if rates fall you can stay put at the bond's higher fixed rate. Compare rates with those on Government stock.

CHAPTER 16

# National Savings

## FIRST Option Bond

Traditionally National Savings schemes have been directed at non-taxpayers, but its latest saving plan is a guaranteed investment bond, with the tax deducted at source. FIRST actually stands for Fixed Interest Rate Savings Tax-Paid. The rate is guaranteed for a year, when savers have the option of either continuing with the investment for another 12 months, at the then guaranteed interest rate, or encashing the bond.

**Suitable for** Taxpayers, although non-taxpayers will be able to reclaim the tax paid on the interest.

**Open to** Anyone over the age of 16. Joint holdings are accepted and trustees can hold them for personal beneficiaries.

**Min–Max** £1,000–£250,000. There is no "topping up" as each purchase is a separate bond.

**Charges** None.

**Withdrawals** In whole or in part of any anniversary date; no notice period is required. However, if the bond is cashed before the first anniversary, no interest will be paid. Thereafter withdrawals between anniversaries would attract half interest for the period from the previous anniversary.

**Interest** Guaranteed at the time of purchase for 12 months, and added to the capital at each anniversary. The current rate is 4.5% net (6.0% gross); an investment of £20,000 plus earns a bonus of 0.3% net (0.4% gross) after 12 months.

**Tax** Basic rate tax is deducted at source before the interest is credited to the bond. Non-taxpayers or those liable to 20 per cent tax will be eligible for a tax refund. Higher rate taxpayers will pay more.

**Children** Not until age 16.

**How to invest** Direct from National Savings, Glasgow, G58 1SB. Forms are available from post offices or ring, free, 0800 88 11 88.

**Record** Certificate.

**Money Mail Rating** *****

**Comment** After the first year, the bond is a relatively flexible addition to the National Savings repertoire. While the Government continues to need to raise funds from National Savings, the interest rate structure should remain quite attractive.

# Capital Bond

Series "H"

A lump sum investment with a low minimum required. It is similar in format to National Savings Certificates but interest is paid gross, and is taxable in the hands of basic and higher rate taxpayers. Interest, which is accumulated, is calculated daily and added on to the bond annually. Designed as a five year investment. Tax, however, has to be paid annually.

**Suitable for** Non-taxpayers, children's savings and basic rate taxpayers who can leave their savings locked up for five years.

| | |
|---|---|
| Open to | Anyone. |
| Min–Max | £100–£250,000 (including total holdings in Capital Bonds since Series "B"). |
| Charges | None. |
| Withdrawals | In full, or partial withdrawals in multiples of £100 providing a balance of £100 retained. |
| Interest | Calculated daily, accumulated before tax annually and fixed at set rates for five year term. At the end of year one: 4.9 per cent, year two: 5.45 per cent, year three: 7.3 per cent, year four: 8.4 per cent, year five: 10.29 per cent (all gross rates) giving gross compound interest rate of 7.25 per cent a year. The net return to basic rate taxpayers is 7.25 per cent. |
| Tax | Interest is accumulated gross, and has to be declared on your tax return each year although payment won't be received until the bonds are encashed. |
| Children | Yes. Withdrawals to parents or designated trustees can be made on their behalf if under age seven and bonds have matured. |
| How to invest | Application forms are available at any post office. |
| Record | Certificate. |
| Money Mail Rating | ***** |
| Comment | Definitely for savers who can last the five year course. This issue is more attractive than its predecessor. The guaranteed return will look attractive when interest rates begin to fall. |

# Children's Bonus Bond

Issue "F"

A new lump sum savings for children under 16 years (who can hold them until age 21). It is a fixed rate, tax-free investment with a return of 7.35 per cent, turning £100 into £142.56, provided the bond is held for the full five years. It is important to keep the bond for five years. Interest is added at the rate of only 5 per cent a year; the real kick comes from the 14.92 per cent final bonus.

| | |
|---|---|
| Suitable for | Children under 16 (at time of investment). |
| Open to | Children under 16. |
| Min–Max | £25–£1,000. |
| Charges | None. |
| Withdrawals | Minimum £25. One month's notice is required for early repayments. No interest is encashed within the first year. |
| Interest | Fixed; 5 per cent a year plus final bonus of 14.92 per cent, making a compound annual return of 7.35 per cent if held for the full five years. |
| Tax | Tax free. |
| Children | Yes. |
| How to invest | Application form at post offices. By anyone over the age of 16 on behalf of an individual under 16. |
| Record | Certificate. |
| Money Mail Rating | ***** |
| Comment | A very attractive return. A must for generous grandparents or relatives. But keep the bond for five years to get the maximum benefit. Suitable as a gift from |

a parent, as the tax-free interest does not (if it exceeds £100) have to be aggregated with the parent's income for tax purposes.

# Deposit Bond

(withdrawn from sale on 19 November 1988)

A lump sum investment. Interest accumulates. There are surrender penalties on early encashment. Terms and conditions are guaranteed for 10 years.

**Charges** None.

**Withdrawals** In multiples of £50, provided £100 remains, subject to three months' notice. Interest payable is reduced to half if the bond is encashed in the first 12 months. Repayment forms and post-paid envelopes are available on request at post offices. Payment is by warrant, treat as a cheque.

**Interest** Variable, at six weeks' notice; calculated daily, credited on anniversary of purchase. Current rate: 6.5 per cent.

**Tax** Not deducted, but interest is taxable and should be declared on tax return.

**Children** No withdrawals if a child is under seven; withdrawals after seven will require child's signature.

**Money Mail Rating** *****

**Comment** The return on Capital Bonds (designed to replace the Deposit Bonds) is currently lower in the first two years, and the same in the third year, so don't switch out of your Deposit Bonds unless you are definitely a long-term holder.

# Income Bond

A lump sum investment paying interest without deduction of tax at source. Interest is variable and usually competitive; it changes less frequently than bank interest rates. There are surrender penalties on early encashment.

## Suitable for

Retired people and others needing a steady flow of income who do not need immediate access to their capital. Non-taxpayers in particular benefit from the gross interest payment and the convenience of monthly income.

## Open to

Anyone.

## Min–Max

Buy in multiples of £1,000; the minimum investment is £2,000, the maximum £250,000.

## Charges

None.

## Withdrawals

In multiples of £1,000, provided £2,000 remains invested, subject to three months' notice. Interest is reduced to half if a bond is encashed within the first 12 months. Repayment forms and pre-paid envelopes are available on request at post offices.

## Interest

Variable, at six weeks' notice; paid on the 5th of the month direct to a bank, building society or National Savings Bank, or by crossed warrant (treat as a cheque). The first interest payment is made after the bond has been held for six weeks and includes all interest due from date of investment. Rate: 6.5 per cent gross. Rate for investments of £25,000 or more, 6.75 per cent gross.

## Tax

Not deducted, but interest is taxable and should be declared on your tax return.

## Children

Yes; but not suitable.

## How to invest

Application forms available at post offices or by post from National Savings and Stock Office, Blackpool FY3 9YP, or by telephone: 0253 697333.

**Record** Certificate.

**Money Mail Rating** *****

**Comment** Gross monthly income is attractive, but if you are a taxpayer the tax will have to be paid; pensioners close to the income ceiling limit for age allowance (see page 31) will find total income calculations easier than investments paying interest in tax-paid form. Although interest is variable it is not likely to rise substantially (it can also fall): some investment providing rising income is also desirable.

# Investment Account

A National Savings Bank account using post office counters paying a competitive interest rate, although it changes less frequently than other banks' interest rate. Interest, which does not have tax deducted at source, accumulates.

**Suitable for** Non-taxpayers including children who do not require immediate access to their funds; for irregular savings of different amounts.

**Open to** Anyone.

**Min–Max** Any amount of £20 or more for each deposit. Maximum investment of £100,000 does not include interest credited to the account.

**Charges** None.

**Withdrawals** One month's notice from the date your application is received at National Savings Bank HQ paid by crossed warrant (treat as a cheque) or cash at a named post office. Repayment forms and pre-paid envelopes are available on request at post offices.

**Interest** Variable; automatically credited to accounts on 31 December. Bank books should be sent to National Savings Bank, Glasgow G58 1SB, to have interest entered. Annual interest statement is available on request. Current rate up to £500: 5.25 per cent; £500+: 5.75 per cent; £25,000+: 6.00 per cent gross.

**Tax** Not deducted, but interest is taxable and should be declared on your tax return. The National Savings Bank has to inform the Inland Revenue of interest paid on each account.

**Children** Yes, but no withdrawals for under-sevens. Investment can be made by parents as trustee when the same conditions apply; withdrawals after seven will require the child's signature as well. Relatives or friends can open an account in a child's name; no withdrawals under the age of seven, afterwards the child can withdraw on own signature.

**How to invest** Application form at post offices; fill in a form at the post office for subsequent deposits. "Save-by-Post" service is available: write to National Savings Bank, Glasgow G58 1SB, or ring free 0800 100 100. Dividends from shares and Government stock can be credited directly to the account.

**Record** Bank book.

**Money Mail Rating** *****

**Comment** Not a substitute for a high-interest cheque book account; judge on investment rather than banking merits. Gross interest payments are attractive. The moderately complicated withdrawal procedure prevents casual usage, for example, by children for whom the account is particularly suitable. It takes longer to get interest credited in January than at any other time of the year, and there is nothing to be gained by sending the bank book off so early.

# Ordinary Account

A two-tiered bank account using post office counters offering modest interest, partly tax free, easy access to funds and some banking services.

**Suitable for** Day-to-day money management of people who either have no bank current account or are frequent users of the post office, for example to draw a pension or other benefits. Higher rate taxpayers who benefit from the partly tax-free interest.

**Open to** Anyone.

**Min–Max** £10–£10,000.

**Charges** None.

**Withdrawals** Up to £100 on demand at any post office, but if over £50 is withdrawn the bank book is kept for checking. "Regular Customer Account" permits up to £250 in cash a day at one chosen post office where you have been a customer for a least six months. Written applications are required for larger withdrawals; forms and pre-paid envelopes are available on request at post offices.

Bills normally paid at the post office e.g., TV licence, road tax – totalling not more than £250 at a time can be paid directly from the account.

**Interest** Provided the account is open for the full calendar year, investors earn a guaranteed 3.25 per cent for each calendar month that there is £500 or more in the account, otherwise 2 per cent. No interest is payable on the month in which the investment or withdrawal is made.

**Tax** Not deducted at source and as partly taxable it should be declared, in full, on your tax return. The first £70 of interest is tax free (capital required £1,400).

**Children** Yes, but no withdrawals for under-sevens; relatives or friends can open an account in a child's name but no withdrawals under seven; afterwards a child can withdraw on own signature.

**How to invest** Application form at post offices; fill in a form at the post office for subsequent deposits.

**Record** Bank book.

**Money Mail Rating** *****

**Comment** Alternative to bank current account for people who want instant record of transactions. If you cannot keep £500 in the account, a building society ordinary account will pay more even if interest is paid net of tax; with £500 or more, a building society cheque or cash card account will usually pay more and offer some banking services too. Higher rate taxpayers no longer benefit from keeping their maximum £1,400 (for tax-free interest).

# 7th Issue Index-Linked Certificates

A lump sum investment, popularly known as "Granny Bonds" (before the new Pensioners Guaranteed Income Bond was launched in 1994), for small to medium-sized amounts which will both grow in line with increases in the cost of living, as measured by the Retail Prices Index, and earn guaranteed interest each year. Certificates have to be held for 12 months to qualify for index-linking. The repayment value of certificates is published each month in the press and listed in post offices. This latest issue has a low scale of annual bonuses, although the final compound bonus is attractive.

**Suitable for** Most investors when the rate of inflation looks set to increase, but more suitable for higher rate taxpayers than non-taxpayers.

**Open to** Anyone.

**Min–Max** Minimum of £100, bought in units of £25; maximum £10,000 (400 units). This is in addition to any other holdings, index-linked and conventional, of National Savings Certificates. A further £20,000 from matured issues of other certificates (index-linked or conventional) and Yearly Plan can be invested in this issue.

**Charges** None.

**Withdrawals** Eight working days' notice is required. Repayment form and pre-paid envelope are available at post offices. Partial withdrawals are permitted. If withdrawn in first year, money back only without interest.

**Interest** Guaranteed for five years. Index-linking is added at the end of the first year on the anniversary of purchase and thereafter the value of certificates moves in line with changes in the Retail Price Index. Extra, guaranteed interest is added.

At the end of year one, interest of 1.25 per cent of the purchase price is added. At succeeding anniversaries the interest is calculated on the value of the bond (including indexation and earlier interest) twelve months before. For example, interest at the end of year 2 is calculated on the value of the bond at the end of year one. Interest added at year two is 1.75 per cent; 2.5 per cent, year three; 3.5 per cent, year four; and 6.07 per cent at the end of year five. The compound annual interest rate is 3.0 per cent, on top of index-linking, over five years. After year five, index-linking will continue and variable rate interest will be paid.

**Tax** Free of income tax and capital gains tax and need not be declared on your tax return.

**Children** Yes, but children have to be aged over seven before certificates can be encashed other than in exceptional circumstances, such as great hardship. Certificates held in trust do not count towards the individual's own maximum investment.

**How to invest** Most post offices and banks have application forms. Quote your holder's number if you have one.

**Record** Certificate. A holder's card which has registered number under which all certificates are held is issued at first purchase of any certificate. This number is quoted on all certificates of whatever issue is bought.

**Money Mail Rating** *****

**Investor protection** Guaranteed by Government.

**Comment** Higher rate taxpayers should top up their holding of tax-free certificates. Provided certificates are held for 12 months, a fairly flexible form of savings.

# 41st Issue Savings Certificates

A lump sum investment for modest amounts which should be held for five years to obtain the maximum benefits, which are tax free, although earlier withdrawals are possible.

**Suitable for** Long-term savings, gifts to children. Particularly attractive to higher rate taxpayers: non-taxpayers should avoid.

**Open to** Anyone.

**Min–Max** £100 (four units); maximum £10,000, but savers of matured issues of savings certificates, including index-linked certificates, can reinvest up to £20,000 of the proceeds in this issue.

**Charges** None.

**Withdrawals** Any number of units. Repayment forms and pre-paid envelopes are available at post offices; allow two weeks for repayment either by warrant (treated as a cheque) or cash at the post office.

**Interest** If held for the full five years, the compound annual rate of interest works out at 5.4 per cent a year. No interest is paid until the end of the first year, thereafter it is paid at three-monthly intervals. At the end of year one, 3.65 per cent is added; 4.05 per cent at the end of year two; 5.4 per cent year three; 6.4 per cent year four; and 7.55 per cent at the end of year five. Investors cashing in "reinvested certificates" in the first year will receive interest, at the rate of 3.65 per cent a year, for each complete three-month period.

**Tax** The interest is tax free and need not be declared on your tax return.

**Children** Suitable for gifts to children; certificates in a child's name cannot be encashed until the child is seven.

**How to invest** At your local post office. If it is a second or subsequent purchase of certificates (any issue), you will need your holder's number card.

**Record** Certificate. If it is your first purchase of certificates you will be given a holder's number card which covers all future purchases of certificates you might make. Quote this number for subsequent purchases or any withdrawals.

**Money Mail rating** *****

**Investor protection** Guaranteed by the Government.

**Comment** Higher rate taxpayers should keep their National Savings Certificates topped up. If you think interest rates are going to fall, exercise the option to convert matured holdings into the 41st Issue. Theoretically, if you think interest rates will rise in the next five years, then the variable General Extension Rate interest earned on mature issues offers more flexibility for switching. In practice, the rate is so low (3.51 per cent) it is not worth keeping any money at this rate.

# Premium Bond

In effect, a money-back lottery ticket. About £3,027 million is invested in Premium Bonds. Once a month ERNIE (Electronic Random Number Indicator Equipment) picks out at random over 190,000 £1 bond numbers which will win prizes ranging from £50 to a "jackpot" of £1 million. From April 1994 there will only be monthly prizes. Every prize winner is notified by post; the post office lists all the winning numbers and big prize numbers are published in the press.

**Suitable for** Anyone wanting a flutter without losing his or her stake money. Tax-free winnings, if any, are attractive for higher rate taxpayers. An alternative to cash gifts.

**Open to** Anyone.

**Min–Max** £1 bonds sold in multiples of £10, minimum investment £100; maximum £20,000. Bonds have to be held for one clear calendar month before being eligible for the draw. Winners of £50 Premium Bond prizes will be able to reinvest their prize warrants despite the £100 minimum transaction.

**Charges** None.

**Withdrawals** Money back only. Partial withdrawals in £10 multiples are allowed. Repayment forms and pre-paid envelopes are available at post offices. Allow eight working days before repayment either by crossed warrant (treated as a cheque) or cash at post offices.

**Interest** None. The prize fund is currently calculated at 5.2 per cent of total money invested in Premium Bonds.

**Tax** Prizes are free of income tax and capital gains tax and need not be declared on your tax return.

**Children** Under the age of 16 bonds must be bought by a parent, guardian or grandparent to whom any prize money will be paid.

**Record** Bond which is issued with individual holder's numbers.

**Money Mail Rating** *****

**Investor protection** Guaranteed by the Government.

**Comment** The odds on winning any prize are 11,000 to 1 – and there are many more £50–£100 prizes than there are big ones. A single bond in the minimum multiple of £10 has as much chance of winning as one from a block of £10,000. There are unclaimed prizes worth over £10 million at 1 April 1993. Are any of them yours?

# Save As You Earn (SAYE)

4th Issue Series "F" Share Option Scheme

A regular monthly savings linked to a company share option scheme. Employees are offered the option to buy shares at a price fixed at the start of the five year savings period which cannot be less than 80 per cent of their current market value. Employees invest a set amount each month in the SAYE scheme. At the end of five years they can either use the money to exercise the share option or take the money with a bonus. They can leave the money invested for another two years to obtain a higher bonus BUT they will then lose the share option entitlement. However, some employers offer a seven year share option plan when the share option can then be exercised.

Interest in the SAYE accumulates tax free. In addition there is a bonus of 9 months' payments tax free at the end of five years, or 18 months' if you leave the savings in for the next two years.

## Suitable for

Employees who want to build up a share stake in their company.

## Open to

Employers running a scheme fix the eligibility rules, usually determined by length of service with the company. Employees may have more than one share option SAYE scheme, provided the overall monthly contribution does not exceed the maximum.

## Min–Max

£10 a month minimum, £250 a month maximum.

## Charges

None.

## Withdrawals

No partial withdrawals. Reduced interest rate penalties on early withdrawal; no interest in year one; years two to five, 5 per cent. If you die, your executor can either take the amount saved or buy shares at the option price.

## Interest

Fixed. Including the bonus is equivalent to 5.53 per cent over five years; including the enlarged bonus, the rate over seven years is equivalent to 5.87 per cent. It is accumulated.

## Tax

Tax free. Once the share option is exercised, dividends are taxable and there is a potential gains tax liability, based on the actual purchase price of the shares, when you sell them.

**Children** No.

**How to invest** You will be invited by your employer to participate in the scheme.

**Record** Certificate.

**Money Mail Rating** ***** until the share option is exercised.

**Investor protection** SAYE is guaranteed by the Government.

**Comment** A useful way of hedging your bets. If the company's shares have risen since you were granted the option, then you exercise the option and buy the share at the lower price fixed when you began saving. You will have a built-in profit. However, if your company has been less successful and the share price is actually lower than the option price, then take the SAYE proceeds as cash.

# Yearly Plan

A regular savings plan for one year at fixed rate of interest; the plan is then converted into a certificate and if held for a further four years it earns a higher fixed rate of interest. A new yearly plan can be taken out each year: the interest rate on subsequent issues might be fixed at different rates. Interest is reinvested and is tax free.

**Suitable for** Most investors wishing to save regularly who are not put off by this scheme's superficial complexity. To get the maximum benefit the plan should be held for five years in all so savings should be for a build-up of capital in circumstances where you want to know what your savings will be worth five years hence.

**Open to** Anyone.

**Min–Max** In multiples of £5, minimum £20 a month; maximum £400.

**Charges** None.

**Withdrawals** On 14 days' notice; no partial withdrawals are allowed. Repayment forms and pre-paid envelopes are available at post offices. No interest is payable if the plan is encashed within the first 12 months.

**Interest** Fixed. If held for full five years 5.4 per cent a year. Rates are lower if you encash the plan earlier: 3.75 per cent p.a. if held for less than two years; 4.75 per cent if held for more than two but less than four years. If six or fewer monthly payments are made, the interest rate is 3.0 per cent p.a.

**Tax** Free of income tax and capital gains tax and need not be declared on your tax return.

**Children** Parents can invest on behalf of a child under seven, but no withdrawals are allowed until the child is aged seven.

**How to invest** Application forms at post offices, but payment must be by standing order.

**Record** Certificate.

**Money Mail Rating** *****

**Investor protection** Guaranteed by the Government.

**Comment** The fixed rate can be attractive when interest rates in general are falling. This savings plan is not as popular as it sometimes deserves to be.

**For the new Pensioners Guaranteed Income Bonds see Appendix 5.*

CHAPTER 17

# Offshore Savings

## Building Society Account

A handful of building societies now have branches offshore, principally in the Isle of Man, which enable them to pay interest gross to UK investors. There is a range of accounts available including Instant Access, Notice and Term Shares. They tend to have higher minimum investments but otherwise are identical to mainland accounts. Interest, however, is paid without deduction of tax.

**Suitable for** Non-taxpayers including non-working wives who need gross interest to offset against their new personal tax allowance, children and other non-taxpayers. Taxpayers wishing to defer their tax liability on the interest.

**Open to** Anyone.

**Min–Max** Varies from £1,000 to £5,000. No maximum.

**Charges** None.

**Withdrawals** Depends on the type of account: instant access on demand; notice accounts, usually three months; term shares, one or more years.

**Interest** Variable; paid gross either half-yearly or annually. Often marginally higher than similar "onshore" account.

**Tax** Interest is paid without deduction of tax.

**Children** Yes. A parent's signature is required for under-sevens.

**How to invest** Consult your local branch. Most large societies operate offshore accounts for UK residents.

**Record** Passbook.

**Money Mail Rating** *****

**Investor protection** Societies' offshore operations are outside the scope of the Investors Protection Act, but under the Building Societies Act 1986, societies are legally bound to bail out any subsidiary which gets into trouble.

**Comment** These accounts were designed to appeal to non-working wives in the wake of independent taxation. They were set up, in the main, before the 1990 Budget which abolished composite rate tax from April 1991. Now that societies in the UK are able to offer gross interest to non-taxpayers, most investors will probably prefer to stay "onshore", although the offshore rates are often a little higher. Some societies (National and Provincial, Woolwich and Yorkshire) allow you to choose your annual interest payment date either side of 5 April to suit your tax position.

Do not confuse these offshore building society accounts with those designed for non-UK residents only which have always been able to offer gross interest to people not liable to UK tax.

# Currency Fund

Equivalent to a bank deposit account in a foreign currency of your own choice, although the investment method is to buy and sell shares in the fund. It is possible to own shares in a currency fund denominated in any of the major world currencies and other less obvious ones such as the Danish kroner, Singapore dollar or Irish punt, and ECU (European Currency Unit). With the same management group it is possible to switch from one currency to another.

| | |
|---|---|
| Suitable for | Non-taxpayers; investors taking a view on currency values; future holiday funds. |
| Open to | Anyone aged 18 or over. |
| Min–Max | Varies; commonly £1,000. No maximum. |
| Charges | No initial fee; an annual fee of ¾–1¼ per cent. |
| Withdrawals | Up to seven days. |
| Interest | Variable; paid gross half-yearly or annually in either foreign currency or sterling if the fund is a "distributor" fund. Interest is reinvested if the fund is an "accumulation" fund. |
| Tax | With a distributor fund the income is paid gross and UK taxpayers must declare and pay income tax on the distribution. With an accumulation fund, the interest is rolled up in the fund without deduction of tax, but when the UK investor realises his profit he will pay income tax on the entire capital gain (which includes any currency appreciations as well as reinvested income). |
| Children | Not suitable. |
| How to invest | Check investment performance in specialist publications such as *Money Management.* Prices and addresses of management companies are quoted on the Offshore Funds page of the *Financial Times.* |
| Record | Share certificate. |

**Money Mail Rating** **!!! to *!!!!

**Investor protection** Regulations have changed from an investor protection point of view. Offshore tax havens such as the Isle of Man, the Channel Islands and Bermuda are now designated territories which means that each has a supervisory system similar to the UK's, including a compensation scheme. Individual funds which are marketed in this country have to be recognised. Either the management company must belong to a regulatory body (for example LAUTRO) or the individual fund must be regulated by the Securities and Investments Board.

**Comment** As managers can obtain a higher interest rate on the large sums (the investors' pooled shareholdings) they have to invest, a single currency fund is an attractive alternative to an individual foreign currency deposit account.

"Managed" currency funds are also available where the investment manager chooses a basket of currencies for you, switching between them depending on the relative outlook for each currency.

# High Interest Cheque Account

An interest-bearing current account, usually with a minimum starting investment, at a bank or branch of a UK bank in the Channel Islands or Isle of Man. It operates in the same way as a domestic high interest cheque account but with the interest paid gross, not net. Most banks stipulate a minimum cheque withdrawal; direct debits and standing orders may be permitted; no overdraft facilities.

**Suitable for** It is a complementary account to a current account; the gross payment of interest may have cash flow attractions to taxpayers, who will pay the tax later.

**Open to** Anyone aged 18 or over (20 in Jersey).

**Min–Max** £1,000–£2,500. No maximum.

| | |
|---|---|
| Charges | Limited number of free cheques at most banks, subsequent ones commonly cost 50p each. |
| Withdrawals | With a few exceptions, minimum cheque withdrawal of £200–£250. |
| Interest | Variable, paid into the account quarterly, half-yearly or annually without deduction of tax. |
| Tax | UK investors declare and pay income tax on the interest. |
| Children | Not unless the account is held in an adult's name. |
| How to invest | Obtain the address of an offshore subsidiary from your local branch of Bank of Scotland, Barclays, Cater Allen, Lloyds, Midland, National Westminster and TSB. |
| Record | Bank statements. |
| Money Mail Rating | ***** |
| Investor protection | No deposit protection scheme, so it is essential to choose a bank which is a subsidiary of a UK bank or well known internationally. |
| Comment | Consider it as an alternative to a domestic high interest current account or instant access building society account. |

# Managed Currency Fund

A lump sum investment through the purchase of shares in a professionally managed fund based outside the UK which invests in a range of cash deposits and other monetary investments (called "instruments") such as bills, in a variety of foreign currencies. It effectively operates like a unit trust with the hoped-for gain coming not from appreciation in share prices, but from one currency rising in value against another.

**Suitable for** Investors who want to hold assets abroad, but do not want to select which currency to hold their money in; non-taxpayers, but there are only marginal tax advantages for UK taxpayers.

**Open to** Anyone aged 18 or over.

**Min–Max** Usually £1,000; no maximum.

**Charges** Initial fee of 3–4 per cent; annual fee of ¾–1¼ per cent.

**Withdrawals** Up to seven days.

**Interest** Variable, paid either half-yearly or annually if the fund has "distributor" status; or accumulated in an accumulation fund. In both cases interest is paid without deduction of tax at source, but the tax treatment differs.

**Tax** Offshore currency funds are either "distributor" funds or "accumulation" funds. With a distributor fund, the income is paid out gross and UK taxpayers declare and pay income tax on the distribution. With an accumulation fund, the interest is rolled up in the fund without deduction of tax, but when the UK investor realises his profit he will pay income tax on the entire capital gain (which includes any currency appreciation as well as reinvested income) he has made.

**Children** Must be held on behalf of a child in an adult's name.

**How to invest** Consult specialist publications such as *Money Management* for performance records and companies' addresses. Prices and addresses are also listed on the Offshore Funds page of the *Financial Times*.

**Record** Share certificate.

**Money Mail Rating** **!!! to *!!!!

**Investor protection** Regulations have changed from an investor protection point of view. Offshore tax havens such as the Isle of Man, the Channel Islands and Bermuda are now designated territories which means that each has a supervisory system similar to the UK's, including a compensation scheme. Individual funds which are marketed in this country have to recognised. Either the management company must belong to a regulatory body (such as LAUTRO) or the individual fund must be regulated by the Securities and Investments Board.

**Comment** Check whether the fund has "distributor" status or not. Among UK banks and unit trust management companies with offshore funds are Guinness Flight, Hill Samuel, INVESCO, Old Court (a Rothschild company), Prudential, N. M. Schroder and TSB.

# Term Account

A lump sum, fixed term, fixed interest rate investment with money tied up for one to five years, in a bank or deposit taker in the Channel Islands or Isle of Man. Interest is paid without deduction of tax.

**Suitable for** Anyone taking a view that interest rates elsewhere will fall.

**Open to** Anyone.

**Min–Max** £100–£5,000 minimum; there may be a maximum, typically £50,000.

**Charges** None.

**Withdrawals** At end of term, other than in exceptional circumstances. There is usually an interest rate penalty for early withdrawal.

**Interest** Fixed; paid without deduction of tax. Higher rates are sometimes negotiable for larger sums. For shorter term investments interest is payable at maturity, otherwise half-yearly or annually.

**Tax** UK investors declare and pay income tax on the interest.

**Children** Not suitable.

**How to invest** Obtain addresses of offshore subsidiaries from UK banks.

**Record** Statement.

**Money Mail Rating** *****

**Investor protection** No compensation scheme, so it is essential to choose a bank which is a subsidiary of UK bank or deposit taker.

**Comment** Short-term cash flow attractions for taxpayers who defer the tax liability. Compare the gross equivalent interest rates of the fixed interest investments where interest has tax deducted at source.

# Unit Trust

A lump sum investment in a professionally managed pool of money which is invested in a wide spread of shares, stocks and other assets. It is similar to a UK authorised unit trust, but because it is based offshore comes under different regulations. Funds from "designated" territories – the Channel Islands, Bermuda and the Isle of Man – now operate under a similar system to the UK's if the funds are marketed over here, and a similar compensation scheme applies.

UCITS have been available since October 1989. The acronym stands for Undertaking for Collective Investments in Transferable Securities and is the invention of the European Commission to cover all forms of collective investments, such as unit trusts, offered by individual Common Market countries to investors in EC member states. Provided individual investment schemes, such as a unit trust, match the rules of a UCITS, then they can be marketed freely.

UCITS marketed in this country have to be registered and follow the UK's investor protection rules, but there is not a compensation scheme to fall back upon.

UCITS can invest in transferable securities such as shares and fixed interest investments, and put up to 5 per cent of their funds into other collective investment schemes.

**Suitable for** Investors wishing to transfer funds outside the UK or to keep foreign-earned assets abroad.

**Open to** Anyone.

**Min–Max** Varies. Commonly £500–£1,000. No maximum.

**Charges** Initial fee of 5–8½ per cent; an annual fee of ½–1 per cent.

**Withdrawals** Usually on demand at market price, sometimes at one month's notice.

**Interest** Variable; paid as a dividend half-yearly without deduction of tax.

**Tax** UK investors declare and pay income tax on the dividend and are liable to capital gains tax on profits at disposal.

**Children** Not suitable.

**How to invest** Check specialist publications such *Money Management* for performance records. Prices and addresses of management companies are listed on the Offshore Funds page of the *Financial Times*.

**Record** Certificate.

**Money Mail Rating** **!!! to !!!!!

**Investor protection** It is important to remember that the investor protection rules (see page **119**) for both UCITS and offshore unit trusts only apply to those funds which are marketed in the UK, either by a financial adviser or the management company itself, say, through press advertising. If you apply direct to the management company yourself, wherever it is based, they will not apply. It will always be sensible to stick to investments run by subsidiaries of established UK companies or those which are well known internationally.

## Comment

From the pure investment point of view for a UK taxpayer there is little to choose between a UK unit trust and an offshore one. Much more depends on the motive or need to keep assets offshore.

CHAPTER 18

# Pensions

## Additional Voluntary Contributions

A tax-free regular savings plan for at least five years, either linked to your company pension scheme or quite separate from it. Your total contributions to your pension scheme and AVC must not exceed 15 per cent of your earnings. All employees who belong to a company pension scheme have the right to make AVC contributions and since October 1987, all employees who belong to a company pension scheme can select their own "free-standing" AVC, outside the firm's pension scheme.

**Suitable for** Anyone who began their pension planning late; last minute boost to retirement income; higher rate taxpayers trying to reduce their tax bill.

**Open to** Anyone who belongs to an approved company pension scheme.

**Min–Max** £5–£10 a month; maximum 15 per cent of your earnings, including mainstream pension scheme contributions on up to a maximum salary of £76,800.

**Charges** Built into life assurance schemes; none with building society AVCs.

**Withdrawals** At retirement, as pension and cash commutation with contracts taken out before 17 March 1987; no commutation permitted on AVCs begun since then. If you change jobs, your existing contributions continue to roll up to provide you with a pension based on their value at retirement. If you die before retirement, a full refund plus interest is made.

**Tax** Premiums get tax relief in full; the pension is treated as earned income, and the commuted cash sum is tax free.

**Children** No.

**How to invest** Your pension scheme manager will advise you of the company's own AVC scheme. If choosing your own free stand (FSAVC) scheme, check the performance of the underlying company in the specialist magazines.

**Record** Annual statement of contributions, AVC value to date.

**Money Mail Rating** Depending on underlying investments ***** to ****!

**Investor protection** Policyholders Protection Act covers 90 per cent of benefits promised by UK authorised insurers provided they are not "excessive". Building society investments are covered by the building society compensation scheme.

**Comment** The best way of boosting future retirement income. If you have been contributing to your company pension scheme for a long time and can expect a pension of two-thirds of final salary or close to that amount, there will not be any point in paying AVCs as your pension, irrespective of how much you have paid towards it, must not exceed two-thirds of final salary. Your pension scheme manager should alert you to this possibility. If you have "over-funded", new rules permit the excess AVCs to be refunded less tax of 35 per cent.

# Personal Pension Plan

A regular savings scheme for pension provision available from July 1988 which can be bought by employees who do not belong to a company pension scheme; employees who belong to a company pension scheme will also have the option of taking out a personal pension plan instead. Personal pension plans are in effect a refinement of and will have many features in common with Self-Employed Retirement Annuities. The totally new feature is the concessions which will be available to employees taking out a personal pension plan instead of remaining in the State Earnings Related Pension Scheme (SERPS) to which all employees not in a company pension scheme automatically belong. Employers, if they wish, can contribute to your personal pension plan. Building societies and unit trust groups are able to offer personal pensions, as well as insurance companies.

## Suitable for

Younger, mobile employees, particularly if their company agrees to contribute to the personal pension. The self-employed. House purchase with a pensions mortgage. Older employees who are currently in a company pension scheme are unlikely to benefit.

## Open to

Self-employed and employees not in a company pension scheme.

## Min–Max

With a few plans the minimum can be as low as £10 a month (which won't buy you much pension). The maximum is effectively £10,500 (up to age 35), more if older, as contributions are limited to earnings of £76,800. In addition to your contributions, and possibly your employer's, the Government, in some circumstances, will make a contribution too. Employees leaving SERPS to take out a personal pension plan will get the National Insurance rebate for contracting out of SERPS. In addition there is a 1 per cent incentive (up to upper tier earnings) paid into the pension plan for those over 30.

## Charges

Investment in the first one to two years is often in "initial" or "capital" units carrying charges of around 7.5 per cent; thereafter around 0.75 per cent a year.

## Withdrawals

A pension may be taken from age 50. Cash commutation of 20–25 per cent of individual pension "pot".

**Interest** Variable; reinvested.

**Tax** Tax relief in full on contributions of $17\frac{1}{2}$ per cent of earnings up to age 35, 20 per cent of earnings from 36–45, 25 per cent from 46–50, 30 per cent from 51–55, 35 per cent from 56–60 and 40 per cent from 61 years. Pension taxed as income; lump sum tax free.

**Children** No.

**Record** Policy and statement.

**Money Mail Rating** ***** to ****!

**Investor protection** Personal pension plans come under the investor protection framework of the Financial Services Act: separate arrangements exist for those schemes, such as investments in building society deposits, which are not covered by the Act.

**Comment** Employees who are not in a company pension scheme should consider this option carefully. Employees who belong to a company pension scheme should compare the combined contributions level made to the company pension scheme by them and their employers with the proposed contribution level to a personal pension plan. A significantly lower contribution level will almost certainly mean a lower pension.

# Self-Employed Retirement Annuity

Regular savings or intermittent lump savings out of tax-free income towards a retirement pension for anyone who does not belong to an occupational pension scheme, a category which includes employees who do not belong to a company pension scheme as well as the self-employed. These contracts ceased to be available from 1 July 1988 when they were replaced by the new Personal Pension Plan (see page **124**), but it is still possible to continue with an existing scheme and make additional contributions to it. Contributions to retirement annuities are invested in insurance-type contract schemes and grow by the addition of bonuses; others resemble unit-linked insurance. At retirement date, the holder has an "open-market" option to choose the highest available annuity, not necessarily the one provided by the company.

**Suitable for** Self-employed and those not in a company pension scheme; employees who have an additional source of income not covered by the company pension scheme. House purchase with a pension mortgage. Late pension planning.

**Open to** Only to those who took out a plan before 1 July 1988, and who wish to either increase their contributions or carry forward payments for the previous six years.

**Min–Max** Regular premiums £10 a month, single premium £500–£1,000. Maximum depends on your earnings and age. It is 17.5 per cent up to age 50, 20 per cent for 51–55, 22.5 per cent for 56–60 and 27.5 per cent for 61 and over.

**Charges** Built into the contract for with-profits type schemes; initial fees of 5 per cent and annual ¾ per cent with unit-linked schemes.

**Withdrawals** As a pension starting at age 60–75 (the age must be specified at the outset), earlier dates are permitted for special occupations such as money-market brokers and footballers; up to around one-third of the pension fund can be taken as a tax-free cash lump sum but for contracts taken out from 17 March 1987 the sum must not exceed £150,000.

**Interest** Variable; reinvested in the pension fund.

**Tax** Tax relief in full on the premiums is given to the level appropriate to your age. You can carry forward contributions, and obtain tax relief, for the preceding six years and forward one year. The cash lump sum is tax free; the pension is taxed as earned income.

**Children** No.

**How to invest** Consult an insurance broker or ask individual companies for a quote.

**Record** Pensions policy and statements.

**Money Mail Rating** ***** to ****!

**Investor protection** Policies issued by UK insurance companies are covered by a compensation scheme providing 90 per cent of benefits provided they are not "excessive". Intermediaries selling pensions policies must belong to a self-regulatory organisation.

**Comment** Although you cannot start a new Self-Employed Retirement Annuity, you can keep an existing one in force and top it up too. It has two main advantages over personal pension plans: you can take a bigger lump sum out of it – three times the pension after a cash lump has been taken, compared with a maximum of 25 per cent of the pension fund with a personal pension plan; and for policies begun before 1987, the cash lump sum is not restricted to £150,000. However, the amount of tax-free earnings that can be put into a SERA is lower than for personal pension plans (see page **124**).

# Transfer Plan

(or *Section 32 Buy Out Bond*)

All job changers now have the choice of leaving their deferred pension with the ex-employer or taking the transfer value of their pension entitlement either to their new company or to the insurance market to purchase a Transfer Plan, often known as a Buy Out Bond. Some companies might only permit such a transfer in respect of pension rights built up since January 1986, when they were compelled to offer job leavers this choice. The money is invested in an individual account and at retirement age, 60–70, is used to buy either a fixed or rising income pension.

**Suitable for** Anyone changing jobs who belongs to an occupational pension scheme, or who is made redundant.

| | |
|---|---|
| Open to | See above. |
| Min–Max | In practice £1,000; no maximum. |
| Charges | Included in the investment. |
| Withdrawals | At retirement only and as a pension only, apart from a tax-free lump sum cash commutation of up to about one-quarter of your final pension fund. |
| Interest | Variable, and accumulated within the pension fund. |
| Tax | Cash sum commuted is tax free, and the pension in payment is taxed as earned income. |
| Children | No. |
| How to invest | Consult your outgoing pension scheme manager for details of your pension transfer value. Some companies prefer to handle the arrangements; others will be more amenable to accepting your choice of company for the Buy Out Bond. An insurance broker, or possibly the pension scheme manager at your new job, will also be able to give advice. Most insurance companies market Buy Out Bonds, including Equitable Life, Legal & General, London & Manchester, London Life, NPI, Scottish Widows, Standard Life, Sun Life. |
| Record | Policy document. |
| Money Mail Rating | ****! |
| Investor protection | Policyholders' Protection Act covers 90 per cent of insurance benefits provided they are not "excessive". This only applies to authorised UK insurance companies. |
| Comment | Buy Out Bonds commonly provide a higher pension than a deferred pension with your former employer. In many ways, the Personal Pension Plan can be used as a more flexible alternative. However, you should always take advice before moving your pension arrangements. |

If you have a pensions problem, such as a suspected miscalculation of a pension or any other unresolved dispute with your existing or former pension scheme, then the Occupational Pensions Advisory Service can help. It is a charity advised by leading people from the pensions industry, and its services are free to pensioners and employees who have exhausted any discussions with the company pension scheme. It will not advise on any current pensions decision you may be considering – such as to stay with a company pension scheme or opt for a new personal pension plan. Occupational Pensions Advisory Service, 11 Belgrave Road, London SW1V 1RB; Tel 071–233 8080. A pensions Ombudsman scheme to cover all aspects of the pensions industry was launched in spring 1991. Tel: 071–834 9144.

CHAPTER 19

# Shares

## Business Expansion Scheme and Fund (Closed December 1993)

These were a lump sum investment in a single company or housing venture. Tax relief was given at the investor's top rate of tax on investments up to £40,000 a year – provided the investment was not realised within five years. So anyone with a BES of under five years should not dispose of it until that crucial anniversary has been passed.

The BES has been replaced by the Enterprise Investment Scheme (see below).

## Enterprise Investment Scheme

When the Government announced that it would axe the Business Expansion Scheme at the end of 1993, it soon became apparent that some sort of successor scheme for investors to back small, unquoted companies would be needed. The Enterprise Investment Scheme (EIS) was announced in the first November Budget in 1993, and came into effect in January 1994. Unlike BES, the new Scheme does not extend to investment in housing. Limited tax relief is given to investors provided the shares are held for five years.

**Open to** Anyone except employees or shareholders of the company. However, unlike the BES, an investor can become a paid director of the company provided he or she was not connected with it before the EIS shares were issued.

**Suitable for** Long-term investors who are happy to accept the risks as well as the potential rewards of backing small companies; they are particularly suited to "hands-on" investors who might wish to get involved in the running of the company.

**Min–Max** The minimum is likely to be £500 to £1,000. The maximum is £40,000 (including any investment in a BES) in tax year 1993–94; from 1994–95 onwards it will be £100,000. It is possible to carry back half of any amount invested between 6 April and 5 October into the previous tax year, up to a maximum of £15,000.

**Charges** These vary so check any prospectus carefully.

**Withdrawals** At any time, provided you can find a purchaser. If you sell within five years you will lose the tax relief.

**Interest** Few companies are expected to pay dividends within the first five years; if they were to, the interest would be taxable.

**Tax** You can claim tax relief at 20 per cent only on an EIS. Provided the shares are held for five years, you will not be liable to capital gains tax on their disposal; if you end up with a capital loss, you will be able to offset that against gains.

**Children** Not suitable.

**How to invest** Information about companies looking for backers should be available from local Training and Enterprise Councils; Venture Capital Report (0491 579999) and The Capital Exchange (0432 342484).

**Record** Share certificate.

**Money Mail Rating** !!!!!

**Investor Protection** If sponsors are used, they must belong to one of the self-regulatory organisations and investors are covered by the appropriate compensation scheme, to a maximum of £48,000.

**Comment** Not for widows and orphans. EIS is a high risk–high reward investment, most suited to businessmen with capital and maybe time to spare.

# Investment Trusts

An investment collective: individual shareholders' funds are pooled and invested in a professionally managed, well-spread portfolio of stocks and shares. Unlike a unit trust, an investment trust is a publicly quoted company whose shares are quoted on the Stock Exchange and rise and fall in value according to demand. Sometimes shares are traded above the "net asset value", the underlying market value of the underlying portfolio of shares, in which case they stand at a "premium"; often they stand at a "discount", that is are traded below the net asset value. Traditionally investment trusts had very general portfolios; nowadays many of them specialise in certain geographical areas, such as Europe or Japan.

**Suitable for** Long-term investors; smaller lump sums; investors wanting to concentrate on one specific investment area.

**Open to** Anyone.

**Min–Max** Theoretically no minimum, but a stockbroker's commission makes investment in amounts below £500 less worthwhile. No maximum.

**Charges** Stockbroker's commission. Commission fees are now 1.6–1.85 per cent (less for deals over £7,000–£8,000), and often with a minimum of £20–£25.

**Withdrawals** Sell shares in any amount through a stockbroker at current market price. You will receive your money in two to three weeks.

**Interest** Variable, called "dividend" and usually paid half-yearly by cheque or direct to your bank account.

**Tax** Interest is paid net of basic rate tax. The amount deducted, known as the "tax credit", can be reclaimed by non-taxpayers; higher rate taxpayers pay more. Although an investment trust itself is not liable to capital gains tax, gains made by investment trust company shareholders are liable to capital gains tax.

**Children** Shares bought for a child must be registered in an adult's name.

**How to invest** Through a stockbroker or a bank's share-dealing service after asking their advice; consult specialist publications for up-to-date commentary and views on the 200 or so investment trusts available. Unlike unit trusts, investment trusts cannot be sold by off-the-page advertisements.

**Record** Share certificate.

**Money Mail Rating** ***!! to *!!!!

**Investor protection** Most management companies to belong to the Investment Management Regulatory Organisation (IMRO) and investors are covered by its compensation scheme, maximum £48,000.

**Comment** Investment trusts are more complicated than unit trusts because the share price can move independently of the underlying market value of the portfolio, but in the last 10 years investment trusts, on average, have proved more rewarding than unit trusts.

# Investment Trust Savings Scheme

A regular savings scheme for an unlimited period into an investment trust. Monthly contributions are collected and invested at advantageous dealing costs. In addition there is also a dividend reinvestment service (not restricted to the dividend of a specific investment trust) and a facility for making small occasional purchases of investment trust shares either for self or as gift.

**Suitable for** Regular modest savings topped up by occasional lump sum investment. A cheaper-than-average way into the stock market.

**Open to** Anyone.

**Min–Max** £20–£25 a month, £250 occasional lump sum. No maximum.

**Charges** Trust managers are able to negotiate much lower stockbroker buying charges, usually up to 0.2 per cent, for block purchases of trust shares. 50p per transaction.

**Withdrawals** You can sell shares through a stockbroker at current market prices, and, in the majority of cases, at normal stockbroker fees, although managers are increasingly able to offer a special dealing rate on disposals too. You will receive your money in two to three weeks.

**Interest** Variable, called "dividend" and usually paid half-yearly either by cheque or direct to your bank account.

**Tax** Interest is paid net of basic rate tax. The amount deducted, known as the "tax credit", can be reclaimed by non-taxpayers; higher rate taxpayers must pay more. Although an investment trust is itself not liable to capital gains tax, gains made by investment trust company shareholders are liable to capital gains tax.

**Children** Shares bought for a child must be registered in an adult's name.

**How to invest** Apply to an investment trust secretary or manager of a group.

**Record** Share certificate.

**Money Mail Rating** ***!! to *!!!!

**Investor protection** Most management companies belong to IMRO, the Investment Management Regulatory Organisation, and investors are covered by its compensation scheme, maximum £48,000.

**Comment** The number of investment trusts and managements seeking to expand their market with savings schemes is growing. Many of AITC's 292 members are included in savings schemes: some of the best known are run by Alliance, Baillie Gifford, Dunedin, Fleming, Foreign & Colonial, Ivory & Sime and Touche Remnant. Twenty groups are now offering an investment trust PEP on a regular savings basis.

# Ordinary Quoted

Lump sum investments in shares "quoted" on the Stock Exchange. To achieve that status, the company must have been thoroughly vetted by the Stock Exchange to make sure it is well managed and financially sound; this includes a five-year track record and at least 25 per cent of its share capital sold at the time the company came to the market as a new issue. The investor's objectives are rising dividend income and a rising share price. But shares can fall in value too, and companies have failed.

**Suitable for** Long-term build-up of capital; short-term speculation. Although the investor hopes to make a profit out of buying shares, remember that it is a risk investment. Shareholders' perks, where available, are a bonus but not a reason for buying.

**Open to** Anyone.

**Min–Max** Theoretically, one share in a company can be bought. In practice £400–£500 per shareholding is more realistic, and several shareholdings desirable.

**Charges** Stockbrokers' fees are no longer fixed. The most common commission for deals under £7,000–£8,000 is 1.65–1.85 per cent with a minimum fee of £20–£25. Lower fees are charged for larger transactions; commission is not charged on new issues. Most banks and some building societies are building up sophisticated share dealing services.

**Withdrawals** In any amount, at current market price with money back after two to three weeks.

**Interest** Variable, with dividend paid half-yearly by cheque or direct to your bank account. When shares go ex-dividend, about five weeks before the dividend date, the seller not the buyer receives the next dividend should the shares be sold in that period.

**Tax** Dividends are paid net of basic rate tax. The amount deducted, known as the "tax credit", can be reclaimed by non-taxpayers; higher rate taxpayers pay more. Gains made by shareholders are liable to capital gains tax.

**Children** Shares bought for a child must be registered in an adult's name.

**How to invest** The Stock Exchange will provide names of stock-broking firms willing to take on new clients; but you will receive only limited investment advice unless a) you are an advisory client and are charged more, or b) a discretionary client where the broker manages your portfolio without consulting you first (although you will be informed). Most banks are now strengthening their sharedealing services, and High Street share shops (provided backed by well-known firms) are another option. Read the City pages and investment magazines for up-to-date information and advice.

**Record** Share certificate.

**Money Mail Rating** ****! to !!!!!

**Investor protection** Share selling is covered by the Financial Services Act, and investors are covered by a compensation scheme of up to £48,000. This does not provide protection against poor shareholdings but unscrupulous selling of shares.

**Comment** Share investment is fun and rewarding provided you accept the risk that shares can fall in value, and are also prepared to work at your investments by keeping tabs on share prices and events which might affect your shareholding. Otherwise buy unit trusts or investment trusts and let the managers do the work for you. Preference shares, a fixed interest share investment where the shares rise or fall, are rarely recommended.

# Personal Equity Plan

Lump sum or regular savings up to a set limit of £6,000 each year invested in UK shares, companies on the Unlisted Securities Market, unit trusts and investment trusts. Shares quoted in the EU are also now counted as suitable investments for a PEP. Registered PEP managers, often banks, unit trust groups and stockbrokers, offer investors a choice ranging from one to 10 shares, individual share selection, or a mixture of units and shares. Unit trust and investment trusts now qualify for the full £6,000 investment. Rules have been relaxed so the PEPs no longer need to be held for a full calendar year to qualify for tax concessions and dividend income can be paid tax free to the PEP holder (not just reinvested). Switching between shares, tax free, is allowed. In addition investors are able to invest £3,000 into a single-company PEP in addition to their main PEP.

**Suitable for** Long-term build-up of tax-free capital; school fee planning, retirement planning; higher rate taxpayers.

**Open to** Anyone 18 or over who does not have a current year PEP.

**Min–Max** Varies: £25–£30 a month, £250 lump sum minimum; £500 a month, £6,000 lump sum maximum.

**Charges** Initial fee of 1–5 per cent, or £30–£70; annual fees of 1–2 per cent. Additional charges of £20–£35 to attend shareholders' meetings.

**Withdrawals** At any time and at current market value.

**Interest** Variable.

**Tax** Proceeds are free of capital gains tax and dividend income is tax free.

**Children** No.

**How to invest** Offered mainly by banks and unit trust groups. A comprehensive list of PEP managers, their addresses and the investment range and charges of their PEPs is published in the *PEP Investor. PEP Guide* lists investment strategy and charges. You need to know your National Insurance number.

**Record** Certificate.

**Money Mail Rating** ***!! to **!!!

**Investor protection** The Financial Services Act covers PEPs, and investors are covered by a compensation scheme of up to £48,000.

**Comment** Capital gains tax does not affect many investors, so this particular tax concession only becomes valuable over the long term when other PEPs have been taken out, but it is a flexible form of regular savings compared with life assurance savings and likely to become increasingly popular, for example, for school fees planning, and linked to a mortgage instead of an endowment policy. Check the charges, particularly the level of annual fees and the dealing cost of shares.

# Permanent Interest Bearing Shares

Permanent interest bearing shares are quoted and traded on the London Stock Exchange. They are issued by building societies and pay an above-average fixed rate of interest but the value of your capital will go up and down with the price. The shares are irredeemable which means the society does not have to repay the principal. The only way you can get your capital back is to sell the shares. How much you get back depends on the market price of the shares, which can go up and down with demand.

**Suitable for** Large investors looking to increase income as part of a portfolio. They are not suitable for savers looking for the best return on their High Street savings.

| | |
|---|---|
| Open to | Anyone. |
| Min–Max | £1,000; no maximum. |
| Charges | You pay commission to stockbrokers on buying and selling. The cost is usually 0.5–0.75 per cent, depending on the size of the deal. |
| Withdrawals | On demand by selling the shares. The proceeds depend on the price at the time of selling. |
| Interest | Paid out half-yearly. Interest payments are non-cumulative so if the society fails to make a payout, it is under no obligation to make the payment at a future date. |
| Tax | Interest is paid net of basic rate tax which can be reclaimed by non-taxpayers. If you sell the shares at a profit, there is no capital gains tax to pay. |
| Children | Not suitable. |
| How to invest | Through a stockbroker. |
| Record | Share certificate. |
| Money Mail Rating | **!!! |
| Investor protection | PIBS are not covered by the building society savings compensation fund. PIBS holders are last in line for a payout if the society is wound up or dissolved. |
| Comment | PIBS are a new type of share issued by building societies. They offer a high fixed interest but, unlike all other building society investments, your capital is at risk. Unlike ordinary gilt-edged securities, PIBS do not have a redemption date when you get your capital back – as a result their market price is extremely sensitive to the level of interest rates. Initially these shares were aimed at huge investors but recent issues allow for a minimum purchase of £1,000. Building societies which so far offer PIBS |

with a low initial investment include Bradford & Bingley (minimum £10,000), Bristol & West, Britannia, Leeds & Holbeck and Skipton, all with a minimum of £1,000.

# Shares quoted on the Unlisted Securities Market

A lump sum investment in the Stock Exchange's junior market, the Unlisted Securities Market (USM). Unlike shares which are listed on the Stock Exchange, companies coming to the USM do not have to be as large, as well-established or release as large a proportion of their shares to the public. With USM companies the minimum trading period is two years and 10 per cent of the capital must be offered. Dividends are sometimes paid, but the object is to invest for capital gain not income. USM shares can be included in Personal Equity Plan portfolios, and many have moved up to a full listing on the Stock Exchange. The Unlisted Securities Market will be closed to new entrants from January 1995 but will continue to trade until the end of December 1996. Discussions are taking place about a replacement for a second or junior market.

**Suitable for** Investors who wish to build up a long-term stake in new companies; higher rate taxpayers actively avoiding income. Not suitable for "widows and orphans". Investors who, if needs be, can afford to lose their money.

**Open to** Anyone.

**Min–Max** Realistic minimum £500; no maximum but with fewer shares available, it is sometimes difficult to buy large amounts.

**Charges** Stockbroker fees of 1.5–1.65 per cent.

**Withdrawals** At market price; there will be a larger spread between the buying and selling prices.

**Interest** Variable, paid net of basic rate tax, and usually low.

**Tax** Higher rate taxpayers must pay more on dividends; non-taxpayers can reclaim basic rate tax deducted; profits are liable to capital gains tax.

**Children** Not suitable.

**How to invest** Through a stockbroker, but ask his advice; check financial pages for press comment about forthcoming newcomers to the USM.

**Record** Share certificate.

**Money Mail Rating** **!!! to !!!!!

**Investor protection** The Securities Association's compensation fund is now in force. The maximum payout is £48,000.

**Comment** The casualty rate of USM companies is not high, but their investment performance has been mixed; the Third Market for even smaller companies only opened at the beginning of 1987 and was closed on 1 January 1991. Consider Enterprise Investment Schemes as a long-term alternative. Never buy unquoted shares in foreign companies, and never buy shares from any organisation outside the UK.

# Unit Trust

An investment collective: individual unitholders pool their money which is professionally managed and invested in a wide spread of shares and sometimes Government stocks. Unit trust prices mirror the value of the underlying portfolio, and like all equity investments can rise or fall in value. Investors have a choice of investing for income, capital growth or a mixture of both; or you can invest in broadly based general funds covering the entire market spectrum either in the UK or overseas, or combining both, or in specialist funds which concentrate on one country or commercial activity. Unit trusts are now available in a wider range of investments including futures and options, warrants and property.

**Suitable for** First time investors in shares; investors wanting to concentrate on one specific overseas investment area; long-term savings for children; investors prepared to sacrifice high immediate income in favour of rising income.

**Open to** Anyone.

**Min–Max** Commonly £500, sometimes £1,000 minimum. No maximum.

**Charges** Initial charge of 3¼–5 per cent built into the "spread", the difference between the buying and selling price of units, which is generally 6–7 per cent. Annual fee of ½–1½ per cent is taken out of the fund's income.

**Withdrawals** Managers have to buy back your units and you will receive the current market buying or "bid" price (the lower of the two quoted) with some groups. The quoted price will no longer be the one dealt at, as new rules permit managers to offer "forward pricing" which means that, like investment in shares, you do not know the exact price until after the deal is concluded. Partial withdrawals are possible if a sufficient minimum balance is retained. Sell by telephone, endorse your unit certificate and return to the manager. You will receive your money about a week later.

**Interest** Variable, called "distribution" and either paid twice yearly or automatically reinvested if the units are "accumulation" units. A few groups offer monthly income based on a set of unit trusts with different distribution dates.

**Tax** Interest is paid net of basic rate tax. The amount deducted, known as a "tax credit", can be reclaimed by non-taxpayers; higher rate taxpayers pay more. Although a unit trust itself is not liable to capital gains tax, gains made by unitholders are liable to capital gains tax.

**Children** Units can be held on behalf of a child and are "designated" with the child's name or initials.

**How to invest** At the beginning of February 1994 there were 156 unit trust management companies running 1,528 unit trusts. Most of these are listed in the national press with addresses and telephone numbers. Managers will send details about any fund. You can buy and sell by phone.

**Record** A contract note itemising your purchase is followed by a certificate once you have paid for the units.

**Money Mail Rating** ****! to *!!!!

**Investor protection** Unitholders' assets are actually held on their behalf by a trustee, usually a major bank or insurance company, formerly approved by the Government but now under the Investment Management Regulatory Organisation (IMRO). In addition each unit trust is authorised by Securities and Investments Board (SIB). The appropriate compensation scheme provides cover up to a maximum of £48,000.

**Comment** There is a wide variation in investment performance. Unless you are actively prepared to manage your unit trust investments, go first for the broadly based unit trust which you can forget about for years. Specialist funds need careful monitoring: last year's winner is frequently this year's laggard. New unit trusts are often offered at a small discount and tend to perform well initially. Study unit trust "form" in magazine and newspaper articles. Watch charges: groups such as Murray Johnstone and Gartmore are spearheading a move to bring down or eliminate initial charges. *Money Management* and *Planned Savings* magazines publish comprehensive performance tables.

# Unit Trust or Investment Trust PEP

Modest lump sum or regular savings investment into a personal equity plan invested exclusively in either unit or investment trusts limited to a maximum of £6,000 a year. The proceeds and dividend income are tax free.

**Suitable for** First time investors; regular savings; higher rate taxpayers in particular.

**Open to** Anyone aged 18 or over who does not already have a current year PEP.

**Min–Max** £25–£50 minimum. The lump sum minimum is usually £1,000 but can be lower; maximum £6,000, or £1,500 if you invest in a fund which has less than 50 per cent of its holdings in UK shares at the moment.

**Charges** Vary. Usually normal unit trust charges and no extras. Others are experimenting with no initial fees, but imposing a charge if you encash the PEP within the first three years. Additional charges of £20–£25 to attend shareholders' meetings.

**Withdrawals** At any time and at current market value; partial withdrawals may be permitted.

**Interest** Variable.

**Tax** The proceeds are free of capital gains tax and interest is tax free.

**Children** No.

**How to invest** Phone or write to unit trust and investment trust management groups for details. Compare charges in specialist publications such as *PEP Investor* or *PEP Guide.* You need to know your National Insurance number.

**Record** Certificate.

**Money Mail Rating** ***!! to **!!!

**Investor protection** The Financial Services Act includes PEPs, and investors are covered by a compensation scheme of up to £48,000.

**Comment** PEPs should be the first form of unit trust investment for most people. Check that there is little or no element of double charging in respect of PEP and unit trust fees.

Remember, you will need to know your National Insurance number when applying for any PEP. Husbands and wives cannot jointly own a PEP, but each can individually take one out.

# Unit Trust Savings Scheme

A regular savings scheme for an unlimited period into a unit trust (see page 141). Flexible: additional savings can be made at any time; savings can be stopped at any time, and either sold in part or together, or held as a lump sum investment. Minimum monthly savings can be very small.

**Suitable for** Savers who cannot afford the minimum lump sum investment in unit trusts; regular savers building up capital from income.

**Open to** Anyone.

**Min–Max** Commonly £25–£30, sometimes £50 a month. No maximum.

**Charges** Initial charge of 3¼–5 per cent is built into the "spread", the difference of 6–7 per cent between the buying and selling price of units. Annual fee of ½–1½ per cent is taken out of the fund's income.

**Withdrawals** Managers have to buy back your units and you will receive the current market buying or "bid" price. Partial withdrawals are sometimes allowed. You will receive your money about a week later.

**Interest** Variable, and either accumulated within the units or used to buy extra units.

**Tax** Interest is paid net of basic rate tax. The amount deducted, known as a "tax credit", can be reclaimed by non-taxpayers; higher rate taxpayers must pay more. Unitholders are liable to capital gains tax.

**Children** Units can be held on behalf of a child and are designated with child's name or initials.

**How to invest** Most of the major unit trust groups run a monthly savings plan; newer groups formed by insurance companies and most of the stockbroker unit trust groups might not have a regular savings plan. Ask managers for an application form.

**Record** Half-yearly statement of interest and the number of units bought each period sent.

**Money Mail Rating** ****! to *!!!!

**Investor protection** Unitholders' assets are actually held on their behalf by a trustee, usually a major bank or insurance company; formerly approved by the Government but now under IMRO, the Investment Management Regulatory Organisation. In addition each unit trust is authorised by SIB, the Securities and Investments Board, which has a compensation scheme providing cover of up to a maximum of £48,000.

**Comment** Regular purchases of units helps to iron out fluctuations in unit prices. Investors who believe in investment cycles should use a savings scheme to buy plenty of units in a specialist fund while the price is low at the bottom of the cycle. Otherwise stick to a general fund for a longer term investment. A unit trust savings scheme may be cheaper, initially, than a monthly savings plan into a unit trust PEP, although over the long term the PEP will probably be the more rewarding investment.

# Venture Capital Trusts

A new form of collective investment announced in the November 1993 Budget designed to back growing and new businesses. Shares will be held in unquoted, smaller companies and investors will benefit from tax-free dividends and capital gains on their holdings. Details of Venture Capital Trusts have yet to be finalised, and the necessary legislation must wait for the 1995 Finance Act, which means that April 1995 looks the earliest these funds could be up and running.

# CHAPTER 20

# Stocks

## Bond Fund

Unit trusts which invest in Government stock and equivalent bonds issued by other Governments overseas are usually described as Bond Funds rather than Bond Unit Trusts. They function exactly like unit trusts, and despite being restricted to fixed interest stocks have shown some strong capital growth too. (When interest rates in general fall, the capital value of Gilts and the like tends to increase.) These funds cannot be linked to a Personal Equity Plan.

**Suitable for** Cautious investors and those who are seeking more rather than less income from their investments.

**Open to** Anyone.

**Min–Max** Varies, but a minimum of £1,000 is common.

**Charges** An initial charge of around 5 per cent is built into the "spread", the difference between the buying and selling price of units. There is also an annual fee of 1–1.5 per cent.

**Withdrawals** On demand, at the lower (or bid) price of the units.

**Interest** Variable, usually distributed half yearly.

**Tax** Distribution is net of basic rate tax; non-taxpayers can reclaim the tax paid, but higher rate taxpayers will pay more. Unitholders are liable to capital gains tax on profits made.

**Children** Units can be held on behalf of a child.

**How to invest** Most management groups advertise their funds in the national press. Alternatively, use the services of an independent financial adviser to recommend a fund which best suits your needs.

**Record** A certificate.

**Money Mail Rating** ***** to ****!

**Investor Protection** Fund management groups are regulated under the terms of the Financial Services Act. A compensation scheme provides cover up to a maximum of £48,000.

**Comment** Bond Funds tend to perform well at different times to funds invested in ordinary shares, so can be a complementary investment to mainstream unit trusts. Their income and safety-first qualities make them an attractive choice for cautious investors, but you cannot get the tax advantages of a PEP with these types of funds.

# Government Index-Linked

Government index-linked stocks are identical to fixed interest Government stocks except in two very important respects. Instead of paying a fixed rate of interest, a modest fixed rate of interest is increased over each six month period in line with increases in the Retail Price Index. At the end of the stock's fixed life span, the nominal value repaid is also increased in line with increases in the Retail Price Index since its issue.

**Suitable for** Anyone wishing to protect their capital from inflation; for higher rate taxpayers, the yields are not high and the stocks are bought for capital appreciation.

**Open to** Anyone.

**Min–Max** See Government Stock.

**Charges** See Government Stock.

**Withdrawals** Any amount at the current market price which will not mirror, at this stage, changes in the Retail Price Index; if withdrawn at redemption, the price will reflect increase in Retail Price Index since the stock was issued.

**Interest** Variable, and will reflect changes in the Retail Price Index over a six month period. See Government Stock for "ex-dividend".

**Tax** See Government Stock.

**Children** See Government Stock.

**How to invest** See Government Stock.

**Record** Stock certificate.

**Money Mail Rating** ***** if held to redemption, otherwise ****!

**Investor protection** Guaranteed by the Government; the Securities Association compensation scheme provides cover up to a maximum of £48,000.

**Comment** In periods of relatively low inflation these stocks have not performed as well as conventional fixed interest stocks, but are likely to improve their rating if inflation rises. National Savings index-linked certificates could be a better medium- to short-term investment although maximum investment is limited.

*Index-Linked Stock*

| | (a) |
|---|---|
| 2% Treasury 1996 | 267.9 |
| 2½% Treasury 2001 | 378.3 |
| 2½% Treasury 2003 | 378.8 |
| 2% Treasury 2006 | 269.5 |
| 2½% Treasury 2009 | 378.8 |
| 2½% Treasury 2011 | 274.6 |
| 2½% Treasury 2013 | 389.2 |
| 2½% Treasury 2016 | 381.6 |
| 2½% Treasury 2020 | 383.1 |
| 2½% Treasury 2024 | 397.7 |

(a) *RPI base month for index-linking adjusted to reflect rebasing of RPI to 100 in January 1987.*

# Government Stock

(commonly called Gilt-Edged Securities)

A lump sum investment in a stock issued by the Government as part of its fund-raising programme. Most stocks are issued with a fixed interest rate and a fixed life span, at the end of which the Government will redeem them in full, at the "nominal" value.

The yield, the return the investor gets from stock at that price, is the yardstick for investing in gilts. If interest rates in general fall, higher-yielding stock will be in demand and the stock price will rise, ultimately driving the yield down; conversely if interest rates are rising, investors will sell their gilts (to get a better return elsewhere) and the price of the stock will fall, forcing the yield up. When you see gilts quoted in the press, you will often see two yields: one is the straight interest/price yield, the other, the "net redemption" yield, takes into account the capital gain or loss, averaged out, that you would make if the stock were held to redemption.

## Suitable for

Most taxpayers, who should buy stocks appropriate to their tax bracket; higher rate taxpayers will be more interested in capital gains while the high yield on other stocks makes them a suitable investment for a retirement portfolio.

## Open to

Anyone.

**Min–Max** Theoretically no minimum, but £250–£500 is more practical in view of the commission to be paid. No maximum, except for stock bought from the National Savings Stock Register where the maximum daily purchase of any one stock is £10,000.

**Charges** On gilts bought from the National Savings Stock Register (via your local post office), the charges are £1 including VAT for purchases of £250 and below, and £1 plus 50p for every additional £125 (or part); on sales the fees including VAT are 10p for every £10 (or part) for deals of less than £100, between £100–£250 £1, over £250, £1, and a further 50p for every additional £125 (or part). This works out at 0.4 per cent. The charges for buying gilts through a stockbroker or bank vary, ranging from 0.4 per cent up to £20,000 to 1.5 per cent up to £5,000. Shop around. There are no charges if you buy a new issue or when the stock is redeemed.

**Withdrawals** Any amount at the current market price; or at redemption date.

**Interest** Fixed, paid half-yearly, net of basic rate tax if bought through a stockbroker or bank, except for War Loan where dividends are always without deduction of tax. If bought from the National Savings Stock Register, dividends are paid gross. Stocks go ex-dividend about five weeks before the dividend date, with the interest going to the seller not the buyer. This is reflected in the price as the interest due to the next dividend date is subtracted from the stock price.

**Tax** Investors are liable to tax on the gross dividend payment from stock on the National Savings Stock Register; higher rate taxpayers must pay more on dividends from stock bought through a stockbroker or bank where basic rate tax is deducted at source; non-taxpayers can reclaim the tax. Gilts are exempt from capital gains tax.

**Children** Stock bought through stockbrokers or banks must be in an adult's name; stock from the National Savings Stock Register can be in the child's name. Children's holdings cannot be transferred to the Bank of England's Stock Register until they are 18.

**How to invest** Through a stockbroker or bank for stock held on the Bank of England Stock Register – this is a comprehensive list. All issues of Government stock are now held on the National Savings Stock Register for which application forms for purchase are available at your post office. The form is DNS 400 (GS1); repurchase forms and envelopes are also available at the post office.

**Record** Stock certificate.

**Money Mail Rating** ***** if held to redemption, otherwise ****!

**Investor protection** Guaranteed by the Government; the Securities Association compensation scheme, providing up to £48,000, is now in force.

**Comment** Dealing through a stockbroker or bank will give you a more immediate price; you might get the next or an even later day's price on purchases from the National Savings Stock Register. But the dealing costs are cheaper and interest is paid without deduction of tax. It is possible to switch from one register to another: obtain the forms from either the Bank of England or Bonds and Stock Office, Blackpool FY3 9YP.

## Loan and Debenture

A lump sum investment in a stock issued by a company at a fixed rate of interest over a fixed period. At the end of the period, the stock is redeemed in full, but until that point the stock is at market prices which can rise or fall. As with Government fixed rate stock, company stock is quoted with a net redemption yield, reflecting any capital gains or losses to be made from that point until maturity, as well as the interest return. Some loan stocks are convertible into ordinary shares at a fixed date and price.

**Suitable for** Most taxpayers whether they want income or capital growth.

**Open to** Anyone aged 18 or over.

**Min–Max**
Realistic minimum £1,000–£2,000; no maximum.

**Charges**
A stockbroker's typical commission is 0.9 per cent on the first £5,000, 0.45 per cent on the next £5,000, less on larger amounts. No fees are levied on new issues or on redemption.

**Withdrawals**
Any amount at market value; or at redemption date.

**Interest**
Fixed, paid half-yearly with basic rate tax deducted. Stock goes ex-dividend about five weeks before interest is paid which means the seller, not buyer, keeps the interest, although the price is adjusted downwards accordingly.

**Tax**
Higher rate taxpayers must pay more, non-taxpayers can reclaim tax deducted. Stocks are exempt from capital gains tax.

**Children**
In an adult's name.

**How to invest**
Through a stockbroker or bank; check convertible options, redemption dates and long-term outlook for the company before proceeding.

**Record**
Stock certificate.

**Money Mail Rating**
***** if held to redemption, otherwise ****! to ***!!

**Investor protection**
If a company fails, debenture holders have a prior claim to be paid in full ahead of other creditors. The Securities Association's compensation scheme, maximum compensation £48,000, is now in force.

**Comment**
Stick to well-known companies; the convertible option can be an attractive way of building up an equity portfolio later.

# Appendix 1

## Shareholder perks

Many companies give perks to shareholders based on the number of shares owned. Some are more attractive and worthwhile than others; but none should be considered as the reason for buying the shares in the first place. Treat the perk as a welcome bonus instead.

The following list, detailing perks by type, and then itemising the individual companies and minimum shareholding to qualify, is based on information supplied by stockbrokers and financial advisers Hargreaves Lansdown.

### Cars – Accessories, Distributors, etc.

**ALEXANDERS HOLDINGS** *Minimum Shareholding: 2,000*
Shareholders' special discount of around 2 per cent is available on any new vehicle bought from one of the dealerships based in Edinburgh, Kirkintilloch, Greenock and Northampton. The discount will be over and above any other discount available. This company is a Ford main dealer.

**KWIK-FIT HOLDINGS** *Minimum Shareholding: 100 ordinary*
Shareholders are entitled to a 10 per cent discount on one purchase of £5 or over. The full price is payable on purchase and a 10 per cent refund will be returned to the shareholder by post.

**LOOKERS GROUP** *Minimum Shareholding: All Shareholders*
Shareholders are entitled to a £100 discount on the purchase of any new motor vehicle purchased from any of the company's garages. This discount is over and above any discounts negotiated in the usual way. The range of vehicles includes Rover, Vauxhall, Ford, Rolls-Royce, Mercedes, VW, Toyota, Renault, Peugeot and Volvo.

**PERRY GROUP** *Minimum Shareholding: All Shareholders*
Privilege purchase terms are available on new cars. These will vary due to market fluctuations and deals will be struck on an individual basis. Perry's also offer a 10 per cent discount on vehicle rental, 10 per cent on car servicing and mechanical repairs and 10 per cent on parts and accessories purchased at a Perry's part shop.

**TRIMOCO** *Minimum Shareholding: 1,000*
A number of discounts are available at Trimoco outlets. These include 2 per cent discount on a new vehicle purchase, £25 discount on vehicle servicing, 10 per cent discount on parts and accessories and 10 per cent discount on vehicle rental.

## Confectionery

**THORNTONS** *Minimum Shareholding: 200 ordinary*
Discount vouchers are sent to shareholders with the annual report each October. In 1991, the value of the vouchers was £21.

## DIY

**MANDERS (HOLDINGS)** *Minimum Shareholding: All Shareholders*
A shareholder's Trade Cash Card can be used at any of the company's 50+ branches and will give discounts of 15 per cent on paint, 10 per cent on sundries and 40 per cent off retail prices for Manders' own wallcoverings.

**MEYER INTERNATIONAL** *Minimum Shareholding: 250 ordinary*
Shareholders are issued with a Jewson discount card entitling the holder to 10 per cent off any purchases, except sale items, from any branch of Jewson. Branches stock a wide range of building materials, timber and other DIY items.

**NORCROS** *Minimum Shareholding: 500 ordinary*
Shareholders are entitled to a 10 per cent discount on purchases of Norcros Group products valued at £20 or more. The discount can be reclaimed after purchase at full price. The following companies are part of the Norcros Group: Building Adhesives Ltd – adhesives, grouts, etc.; Crosby Kitchens – fitted kitchens; Crosby Sarek Ltd – timber doors and windows; H & R Johnson Tiles Ltd – ceramic wall and floor tiles; Triton plc – electric showers, etc.

## Dry Cleaning

**BROOKS SERVICE GROUP** *Minimum Shareholding: 750 ordinary*
Shareholders will be issued with a concession card which entitles the bearer to a 25 per cent discount on dry cleaning, tailoring repairs, shoe repairs and key cutting, and a 50 per cent discount on the cost of carpet cleaning equipment hire. Brooks also run special offers solely for shareholders from time to time, normally during quiet trading periods.

**JOHNSON GROUP CLEANERS** *Minimum Shareholding: 200 ordinary shares/ 1,000 preference shares or CCRP share preference*
Shareholders who are eligible will receive a discount card entitling them to 25 per cent off all dry cleaning at Johnson Group shops. Johnson Group Cleaners group include Johnsons, Smiths, Crockatt Cleaning, Pullars, Bollom and Zernys.

**SKETCHLEY** *Minimum Shareholding: 1,000 ordinary*
A shareholder's discount card is issued which entitles the holder to 25 per cent discount off list prices at Sketchley Cleaners. The card cannot be used at Jeeves of Belgravia or Lilliman & Cox.

## Fashion

**ALEXON GROUP** *Minimum Shareholding: All Shareholders*
Shareholders are issued with a voucher entitling the bearer to a 20 per cent discount on one transaction purchasing goods from any UK Alexon or Dash branch. This cannot be used in conjunction with any other special offer.

**LAURA ASHLEY** *Minimum Shareholding: All Shareholders*
A voucher allowing a 10 per cent discount on one purchase has been sent to shareholders along with the annual report and accounts in the last few years.

**AUSTIN REED** *Minimum Shareholding: 500*
Shareholders can apply for a Shareholder Discount Card which entitles them to 15 per cent discount on purchases of ladies and menswear and most other merchandise at the company's retail outlets. This offer cannot be used in conjunction with any other special offers.

**BURTON GROUP** *Minimum Shareholding: 1,000 ordinary*
A 12.5 per cent discount is available on goods bought in the group's retail outlets using a group chargecard. The reduction is automatically shown on the monthly statement. The group's retail outlets include Burton, Top Man, Principles, Top Shop and Debenhams.

**GIEVES GROUP** *Minimum Shareholding: 600 ordinary shares (held for a minimum of 3 months)*
Shareholders are issued with a card which entitles them to a 20 per cent discount on purchases made in Gieves & Hawkes' UK stores. Goods offered at reduced prices or special promotions are not eligible for further discounts with the shareholder's card.

**HOLLAS GROUP** *Minimum Shareholding: 500 ordinary*
Shareholders are offered 20 per cent discount on goods purchased at the subsidiary company of Hawkshead Sportswear Ltd. The three outlets are in Hawkshead and Grasmere in Cumbria and at 9 Stonegate, York. A 20 per cent discount is also available on an initial order from their catalogue.

**MOSS BROS GROUP** *Minimum Shareholding: 250 ordinary shares (held for a minimum of 6 months)*
Shareholders are entitled to a 10 per cent discount at the company's retail outlets.

**NEXT** *Minimum Shareholding: 500 shares*
A 25 per cent discount voucher valid for the price of all purchases made on one occasion before end June 1992 is sent to qualifying shareholders. It is redeemable at any branch of Next, but excludes Next to Nothing and Next Directory.

**SEARS plc** *Minimum Shareholding: 500 ordinary shares*
Vouchers for use by qualifying shareholders and their immediate family are provided to obtain discounts in all departments of Selfridges, Oxford Street, and orders from the Selfridge Selection mail order catalogue. A total saving of £127.50 against purchases of £850 or more is possible. Sears plc donate 20 pence to Save the Children Fund for every £1 of discount used, up to a maximum donation of £50,000.

## Financial Services

**ABERDEEN TRUST** *Minimum Shareholding: 2,000 ordinary*
Shareholders are entitled to free membership of the Country Gentlemen's Association. The benefits of the Association include an annual diary, the monthly magazine *Country* and various special offers in the areas of travel, wine, etc. All shareholders are entitled to a 2 per cent discount on the purchase of any units in the Abtrust range of unit trusts.

**BANK OF SCOTLAND** *Minimum Shareholding: 1,200 ordinary shares (held for at least 12 months)*
The Bank of Scotland Personal Stockholders Benefits Scheme covers four products: 1) Premier Visa Card – the normal charges are waived for shareholders who comply with the required criteria. 2) One-third off Travel Insurance. 3) 50 per cent discount on normal Bank of Scotland PEP management charges. 4) Bank of Scotland Visa traveller's cheques available at no commission charge.

**BERRY BIRCH & NOBLE** *Minimum Shareholding: 500 ordinary*
10 per cent discount off the premium (after all policy discounts) on any household insurance policies, in respect of your main residence, effected through the agency of a participating company, providing the participating company is informed when a policy is effected or renewed.

**GENERAL ACCIDENT** *Minimum Shareholding: All Shareholders*
Shareholders and their immediate family are entitled to a discount of 10 per cent on home and car policies effected directly with General Accident. The concession is also available on certain life policies

depending on the nature of the contract and length of term.

**INVESCO MIM** *Minimum Shareholding: All Shareholders (held for at least 12 months)*
Shareholders are entitled to a 2 per cent discount on the full range of MIM Britannia unit trust purchases.

## Foods

**ICELAND FROZEN FOODS** *Minimum Shareholding: All Shareholders*
Food vouchers entitling shareholders to £1 off per £10 spent up to £30. A £10 voucher is also issued to be used against the purchase of any freezer, fridge freezer, fridge, microwave or dishwasher costing more than £100 at an Iceland store.

**PARK FOOD GROUP** *Minimum Shareholding: All Shareholders*
Park Food Group offers shareholders a 20 per cent discount on a range of hampers supplied by their subsidiary KUS Ltd.

## Funerals

**GREAT SOUTHERN GROUP** *Minimum Shareholding: All Shareholders*
Discount on Chosen Heritage pre-paid funeral plans.

## Furnishing

**COURTS (FURNISHERS)** *Minimum Shareholding: 100 ordinary shares (held for a minimum of 3 months)*
Shareholders are entitled to a discount of 10 per cent on purchases at Courts retail outlets. This cannot be used in conjunction with any other offer running in the stores.

**EMESS** *Minimum Shareholding: 100 ordinary*
A 33 per cent discount is available on the trade price of selected products from the Cresswell Elite range (exclusively designed tablelamps). The maximum usage of the concession is £500 per annum.

## Health

**COMMUNITY HOSPITALS GROUP** *Minimum Shareholding: 500 ordinary*
Shareholders living near facilities are invited to hospitality events such as the launching of a new service or opening of a new extension. The HealthCheck range of health screens is available at a 20 per cent discount to shareholders. Priority reservations are given to shareholders and close relations. Shareholders admitted to any of the hospitals are welcomed with a hospitality gift pack.

**LLOYDS CHEMIST GROUP** *Minimum Shareholding: All Shareholders*
Two 20 per cent discount vouchers are issued to all shareholders with the company's annual report and accounts. These can be used at any of the group's stores; Lloyds Chemists, Lloyds Supersave Drugstores and Holland and Barrett.

**REGINA HEALTH & BEAUTY PRODUCTS** *Minimum Shareholding: 20,000, or any number of ordinary shares provided they were registered before 6 September 1990*
Shareholders are entitled to a 25 per cent discount on the company's products.

## Hotels

**ANN STREET BREWERY** *Minimum Shareholding: All Shareholders*
25 per cent discount for bed and breakfast for two at St Pierre Park Hotel, Guernsey.

**BURTONWOOD BREWERY** *Minimum Shareholding: All Shareholders*
Discount vouchers to the following values were issued in 1991 and the company intend to make similar offers in the future: £20 off a weekend break package at listed hotels; £12 off a meal for two or more at listed Burtonwood pubs; 2 × £4 off bar snacks for two or more at listed Burtonwood pubs.

**FORTE (formerly Trusthouse Forte)** *Minimum Shareholding: 300 ordinary*
A shareholder concession of a 10 per cent discount is available through either the Forte Gold Card or through Leisure Cheques. If the Forte Gold Card is used the 10 per cent discount will be shown on the monthly statement, not at the outlet. Leisure Cheques can be bought at 90 per cent of their face value and then used at face value, giving a 10 per cent discount.

**FRIENDLY HOTELS** *Minimum Shareholding: All Shareholders*
A Friendly Club card is issued to all shareholders entitling the holder to 10 per cent off accommodation at any Friendly Hotel and 5 per cent off every type of function including conferences and exhibitions.

**THE GREENALLS GROUP** *Minimum Shareholding: All Shareholders*
Shareholders receive 10 per cent off the accommodation tariffs in any De Vere hotel.

**LADBROKE GROUP** *Minimum Shareholding: All Shareholders*
Shareholders are entitled to discounts as follows: 10 per cent off accommodation, food and beverages in overseas hotels; 10 per cent off accommodation, food and beverages in UK hotels; 20 per cent off pre-booked Weekend Breaks; 5 per cent off published conference package tarrifs. Discounts are also given at Texas Homecare centres – 10 × £5 vouchers are issued, with one allowable for every £40 of purchases.

**QUEENS MOAT HOUSES** *Minimum Shareholding: All Shareholders*
The current shareholder concession is for £40 made up of a £25 voucher towards the cost of a Town & Country Classic Weekend Break and 2 × £7.50 vouchers towards food and beverage costs.

**RESORT HOTELS** *Minimum Shareholding: All Shareholders*
Shareholders are sent Privilege Cards entitling them to the following discounts: 15 per cent off Carefree Days (weekend and short breaks) – up to three rooms qualify for the discount for a maximum stay of seven days; 10 per cent off full published rates for accommodation only – max 3 rooms; 10 per cent off meal prices at any Resort restaurant or brasserie. The discount applies only to meals over £5 per head and not to drinks.

**RYAN HOTELS** *Minimum Shareholding: All Shareholders*
The shareholder's discount card entitles the bearer to a 10 per cent discount on all services (excluding bar drinks).

**THE SAVOY HOTELS** *Minimum Shareholding: All Shareholders*
A 10 per cent discount on accommodation at the Savoy, Claridges, the Berkeley, the Lygon Arms and the Lancaster in Paris. The discount cannot be used in conjunction with any other promotional offers.

**SECURICOR GROUP** *Minimum Shareholding: All Shareholders*
The Securicor Group offers shareholders a 10 per cent discount at the group's hotels in Richmond and Coventry and a 5 per cent discount on package holidays booked through Phoenix travel. A free buffet lunch is also provided for shareholders attending the AGM in April.

**STAKIS** *Minimum Shareholding: 300 ordinary*
A Stakis Shareholder's Privilege Card provides a 10 per cent discount on services in Stakis Hotels including accommodation, meals and drinks. A 5 per cent discount is available on most major tour operators' holidays, booked through Stakis plc's own travel agency, Trend Travel. Stakis may also issue discount vouchers giving up to a 30 per cent discount on weekend breaks, city breaks, timeshare, etc.

**VAUX GROUP** *Minimum Shareholding: All Shareholders*
A discount card is issued to shareholders each calendar year. This entitles the bearer to 10 per cent off accommodation and restaurant bills at Swallow

Hotels, 10 per cent off meals at Vaux Inns and 10 per cent off annual membership at Swallow Leisure Clubs. The group also issue vouchers towards the cost of weekend breaks.

## Jewellery

**ASPREY** *Minimum Shareholding: 5,062 ordinary*
An Asprey Card entitles shareholders to a 15 per cent discount on cash and cheque purchases from any of the Asprey Group Stores.

**GOLDSMITHS GROUP** *Minimum Shareholding: All Shareholders*
The company issues its shareholders with 2 × 15 per cent discount vouchers every six months.

**RATNERS GROUP** *Minimum Shareholding: All Shareholders*
A shareholder discount card is issued which entitles shareholders to a 10 per cent discount on all goods and services throughout the UK. Retail outlets include Ratners, H Samuel, Ernest Jones and Salisbury's.

## Leather Goods

**HARTSTONE GROUP** *Minimum Shareholding: All Shareholders*
Shareholders are able to purchase some of the company's leather goods at reduced prices.

**WORLD OF LEATHER** *Minimum Shareholding: 500 ordinary shares (held for a minimum of 6 months)*
A 10 per cent discount is available on all World of Leather products and may be taken in addition to any other offers operating at the time.

## Miscellaneous

**BSG INTERNATIONAL** *Minimum Shareholding: All Shareholders*
Discounts of up to 50 per cent are available on Britax automotive products and childcare products. Contact the Group Secretary, Mr Thorne, for the exact rate on each item. Special terms for car lease and servicing.

**THOMAS JOURDAN** *Minimum Shareholding: 1,000 ordinary shares (held for a minimum of 6 months)*
Discounts are available from the following retail outlets: John Corby Ltd – trouser presses, tie racks, 15 per cent; Lion Brush Works Ltd – artists and cosmetic brushes, approx. 30 per cent; Suncrest Surrounds Ltd – fireplace surrounds and suites, approx. 25 per cent; Unerman Holdings plc – furniture fittings, handles, etc., approx. 20 per cent; Woodstock Furniture Ltd – fitted kitchens, boards, etc., 5–15 per cent.

**LONRHO** *Minimum Shareholding: 100 ordinary*
Vouchers are sent to Lonrho shareholders giving the following discounts: Brentford's, 15 per cent discount on any purchases; Metropole Hotels, 10–30 per cent discount depending on resort. Discounts at Princess Hotels, also off selected goods from Southern Watch & Clock Supplies, and £30 off car servicing at a Dutton-Forshaw dealership.

**PENTOS** *Minimum Shareholding: 500 ordinary*
Shareholders are entitled to a 10 per cent discount in all Pentos retail outlets, i.e. Dillons, Claude Gill, Hatchards, Economist, Athena, Ryman and Wilding.

## Photography

**UPTON & SOUTHERN HOLDINGS** *Minimum Shareholding: 250 ordinary*
Shareholders are entitled to receive discounts on purchases from the company's retail outlets: E. Upton & Sons plc, McKenna & Brown photo/hi-fi, and Brittains of Rotherham in the Cleveland and Yorkshire areas. The discounts available are 10–15 per cent but do not apply to sale goods.

## Property

**BARRATT DEVELOPMENTS** *Minimum Shareholding: 1,000 ordinary shares (held for a minimum of 12 months)*
Barratt shareholders are entitled to a discount of

£500 per £25,000 (or part thereof) on the purchase of a new Barratt property in the UK, USA or Europe.

**BELLWAY** *Minimum Shareholding: 1,000 ordinary shares (held for a minimum of 12 months)*
Discounts are available as follows: 10–15 per cent (depending on the time of year) off car parking in the Bellair Car Port for people flying from Newcastle Airport; 10 per cent off kitchen units from Nixons Kitchens. A discount of £600 per £25,000, or pro rata on part thereof, on the purchase price of a new Bellway house up to a maximum discount of £3,000.

**FIRED EARTH TILES** *Minimum Shareholding: 500 ordinary shares (held for a minimum of 3 months)*
Shareholders are entitled to a 12.5 per cent discount on the company's products.

## Publishing

**EMAP** *Minimum Shareholding: All Shareholders*
Discounted subscriptions to various consumer magazines, e.g. *Practical Photography*, *Garden News* and *Steam Railways*.

## Restaurants

**ALLIED LYONS** *Minimum Shareholding: All Shareholders*
A booklet of vouchers relating to group products and catering establishments is issued to shareholders with the annual report and accounts.

**HARRY RAMSDEN'S plc** *Minimum Shareholding: All Shareholders*
A Shareholder's Card entitles the bearer and one guest to a 20 per cent discount on restaurant meals served from Monday to Thursday inclusive (excluding bank holidays) at any of the company's outlets. Invitations will also be extended to shareholders to functions held at the ordinary Harry Ramsden's in Guiseley – "the world's largest fish and chip shop" – where celebrities will also be in attendance.

**SEFTON HOTEL** *Minimum Shareholding: All Shareholders*
A 10 per cent discount on restaurant meals.

## Retailing

**BENTALLS** *Minimum Shareholding: 100 ordinary*
The company issues shareholders with six discount vouchers together with the annual report and accounts. These entitle shareholders to a £1 to £10 discount against 10 per cent of the bill in any of the company's seven department stores based in London and the South East.

**THE BOOTS COMPANY** *Minimum Shareholding: 100 ordinary*
For the past few years shareholders have been issued with 10 vouchers which will give a £1 discount on any purchases totalling over £5 made in the Group's UK retail stores.

## Security

**BROWN & JACKSON** *Minimum Shareholding: All Shareholders*
Shareholders are offered a free home security survey and a 10 per cent discount on an ATI electronic alarm system.

## Shoes

**STYLO** *Minimum Shareholding: All Shareholders*
Every shareholder is entitled to two 20 per cent discount vouchers for use at Stylo retail outlets. The vouchers are issued with the annual report and accounts.

## Sports

**HAWTIN** *Minimum Shareholding: All Shareholders*
Shareholders are entitled to discount on various Gul Wet Suits.

## Stores

**N. BROWN GROUP** *Minimum Shareholding: All Shareholders*
Shareholders are entitled to a 20 per cent discount on purchases from any of the group's catalogues. Discounts are also available on a range of financial services via Morfitt and Turnbull.

**STOREHOUSE** *Minimum Shareholding: 500 ordinary*
Shareholders are offered a 10 per cent discount on purchases at the group's UK stores of up to £500 worth of merchandise. The discount is offered through vouchers which are dispatched with the company report and accounts in June.

**TOYE & CO** *Minimum Shareholding: 250 ordinary*
A Special Purchase Card is issued entitling the holder to a 15 per cent discount on purchases made at the retail outlets of Toye and Kenning & Spencer Ltd. Shops are based in London, Bedworth, Glasgow and Manchester, and a mail order service is also available for those shareholders not living in close proximity to the stores.

## Travel

**AIRTOURS** *Minimum Shareholding: All Shareholders*
Shareholders are offered a 10 per cent discount on Airtours holidays booked through a special shareholders' holiday advice line. This offer is available on any holidays highlighted in Airtours brochures including the Camping brochure.

**BARR & WALLACE ARNOLD TRUST** *Minimum Shareholding: 500 ordinary or A ordinary*
Shareholders are entitled to the following discounts: 10 per cent off holidays booked through a Wallace Arnold Travel Shop; 5 per cent off at any of the group's four hotels; 10 per cent off new cars purchased at the group's dealerships. If shareholders wish to take up these offers they should contact the company secretary who will issue discount vouchers.

**BRITISH AIRWAYS** *Minimum Shareholding: 200 ordinary*
A coupon is issued to shareholders which entitles the bearer and up to three more family members to 10 per cent off any British Airways published fare, for leisure travel only, from or within the UK, or 5 per cent off the basic price of a British Airways Holiday package tour.

**ISLE OF MAN STEAM PACKET** *Minimum Shareholding: 1,000*
A 50 per cent discount on a return passage ticket; maximum of three discounted tickets. Also, a 50 per cent discount on private car ferry fares.

**P & O** *Minimum Shareholding: varies dependent on type of shares held*
1) Min shareholding – 600 5.5 per cent £1 red. non-cum preferred: a 50 per cent discount Dover to Calais/Boulogne/Ostend and Felixstowe/Zeebrugge; 25 per cent discount Cairnyman to Larne.
2) Min shareholding – 300 5.5 per cent £1 red non-cum preferred: half above discounts, unlimited crossings, private car plus four people, some restrictions at peak hours. Individual shareholders must be on list by the 31 December before sailing date, and still on at time of crossing.
3) Min shareholding – 200 dfd Ord or 500 nominal cum preferred: a 30 per cent discount Aberdeen to Lerwick (Shetland), Scrabster to Strommess (Orkney); all sailings except July and August, subject to availability of space, limit two round trips in 12 months, private car or motorcyle and accompanying passengers (max. four adults). Standard tariff for caravans and trailers.

**THE RANK ORGANISATION** *Minimum Shareholding: 500, or any number of ordinary shares if held for more than 3 years*
A voucher worth £25 is effective from 1 April 1992 and can be used as part payment towards holidays booked from the following brochures: Butlins, Haven, Warner and Shearing. It may also be used towards the cost of accommodation at many of the groups' hotels. The shareholder must be included in the bookings.

**SCANDINAVIAN SEAWAYS** *Minimum Shareholding: 1,000*
A 25 per cent discount for shareholder and one other (but not car) on ferry fares.

**TRAFALGAR HOUSE** *Minimum Shareholding: 500 ordinary*
Shareholders are entitled to discounts of 10 or 15 per cent (depending on length of holiday, etc.) on the full published brochure price of holidays on the *QE2*, *Cunard Countess*, *Cunard Princess*, *Cunard Sea Goddess I*, *Cunard Sea Goddess II* and on Vistafjord and Sagafjord cruises. This offer cannot be used in conjunction with any other.

## Wines and Spirits

**ELDRIDGE, POPE & CO** *Minimum Shareholding: All Shareholders*
Shareholders are offered selected quality wines at around a 10 per cent discount.

**FULLER, SMITH & TURNER** *Minimum Shareholding: All Shareholders*
Shareholders are offered a 5 per cent discount on cases of wines.

**GRAND METROPOLITAN** *Minimum Shareholding: All Shareholders*
Shareholders are normally issued with a booklet of vouchers in January each year. In 1992 they were made an offer of discounted cases of wine delivered free of charge.

**GREENE KING** *Minimum Shareholding: All Shareholders*
Each year shareholders are invited to take part in a discounted case of wine offer. Various wines are offered each year with a discount of 15–20 per cent on normal retail prices.

**MERRYDOWN WINE** *Minimum Shareholding: 190*
Substantial discounts on published wholesale prices of most Merrydown products including ciders, mead, fruit wines, vinegars, honey and preserves. These must be purchased per case and a delivery charge will be added to the price.

**SCOTTISH & NEWCASTLE** *Minimum Shareholding: All Shareholders*
Together with the annual report and accounts, shareholders are sent a discounted offer on two cases of wines and spirits. The offer remains open for around three months.

**WHITBREAD** *Minimum Shareholding: All Shareholders*
Shareholders are sent discount vouchers each year with the annual report and accounts. Last year these vouchers represented a £45 discount when redeemed against total purchases of £300 from named Whitbread outlets. These vouchers may not be used in conjunction with any other offer and are not transferable.

Reprinted by courtesy of Hargreaves Lansdown Stockbrokers, Embassy House, Queens Avenue, Clifton, Bristol BS8 1SB. Freephone: 0800 850 661.

# Appendix 2

## Recent Issues of National Savings Certificates

All the following issues are within the first five years of their life when fixed interest rates (pitched at a competitive level when the issue first goes on sale) apply. Thereafter variable interest is added every three months (see the general extension rate).

The compound rate of interest over the first five years is usually quoted. It is a useful yardstick for making long-term (i.e. five years in this case) comparisons.

As interest payments are not constant but increase towards the end of the term, check both the annual yield and the average return obtained from holding from now until the end of the term for more immediate comparisons.

Once these certificates reach the end of the five year term, variable interest is added every three months – known as the *general extension rate.* This is now below the compound rate of interest on the current issue of certificates and varies. The fixed interest rate extensions to older issues of certificates has been phased out and completely replaced by the general extension rate.

As interest is added either at three-monthly intervals (or four-monthly with older issues) when you cash in your certificates, do so immediately after a payment date. Check the purchase date on the certificates to calculate the interim anniversary dates.

Capital Bonds are not strictly speaking National Savings Certificates, because the interest is not tax free. It is accumulated before deduction of tax which has to be paid annually. However, their format is sufficiently similar to National Savings Certificates to include them in this detailed schedule of rates and values.

**34th Issue**
**Sold at £25 a unit from 22 July 1988 – 16 June 1990**
*Compound interest rate over first five years = 7.5%*

| Year | Interest: 3 monthly† £ | Value anniversary of purchase £ | Yield anniversary of purchase % | Average yield to end term % |
|---|---|---|---|---|
| 4 | 0.64½ | 32.77 | 8.5 | 9.0 |
| 5 | 0.78 | 35.89 | 9.5 | 9.5 |

**35th Issue**
**Sold at £25 a unit from 18 June 1990 – 14 March 1991**
*Compound interest rate over first five years = 9.5%*

| Year | Interest: 3 monthly† £ | Value anniversary of purchase £ | Yield anniversary of purchase % | Average yield to end term % |
|---|---|---|---|---|
| 3 | 0.67¾ | 31.27 | 9.3 | 11.2 |
| 4 | 0.83¾ | 34.65 | 10.8 | 12.2 |
| 5 | 1.01½ | 39.36 | 13.6 | 13.6 |

**36th Issue**
**Sold at £25 a unit from 2 April 1991 – 2 May 1992**
*Compound interest rate over first five years = 8.5%*

| Year | Interest: 3 monthly† £ | Value anniversary of purchase £ | Yield anniversary of purchase % | Average yield to end term % |
|---|---|---|---|---|
| 2 | 0.50 | 28.09 | 6.5 | 9.3 |
| 3 | 0.57½ | 30.41 | 8.3 | 10.2 |
| 4 | 0.73¼ | 33.39 | 9.8 | 11.2 |
| 5 | 0.89¼ | 37.59 | 12.6 | 12.6 |

33rd–36th Issues
* Paid at end of first 12 months.
† Average for quarter if certificates held to next anniversary.

**37th Issue**
**Sold at £25 a unit from 13 May 1992–5 August 1992**
*Compound interest rate over first five years = 8%*

| Year | Interest: 3 monthly | Value anniversary of purchase | Yield anniversary of purchase | Average yield to end term |
|---|---|---|---|---|
| | £ | £ | % | % |
| 2 | 0.41 | 28.02 | 6.2 | 8.7 |
| 3 | 0.56 | 30.26 | 8.0 | 9.5 |
| 4 | 0.71 | 33.10 | 9.4 | 10.2 |
| 5 | 0.91 | 36.74 | 11.0 | 11.0 |

**38th Issue**
**Sold at £25 a unit from 24 August 1992–22 September 1992**
**(38th Reinvestment Issue from 6 August 1992–4 October 1992)**
*Compound interest rate over first five years = 7.5%*

| Year | Interest: 3 monthly | Value anniversary of purchase | Yield anniversary of purchase | Average yield to end term |
|---|---|---|---|---|
| | £ | £ | % | % |
| 2 | 0.40¼ | 27.94 | 6.2 | 8.0 |
| 3 | 0.50¾ | 29.95 | 7.2 | 8.7 |
| 4 | 0.63 | 32.47 | 8.4 | 9.4 |
| 5 | 0.85½ | 35.89 | 10.5 | 10.5 |

**39th Issue**
**Sold at £100 a unit from 5 October 1992–12 November 1992**
*Compound interest rate over first five years = 6.75%*

| Year | Interest: 3 monthly | Value anniversary of purchase | Yield anniversary of purchase | Average yield to end term |
|---|---|---|---|---|
| | £ | £ | % | % |
| 2 | 1.37¼ | 110.09 | 5.3 | 7.3 |
| 3 | 1.85¾ | 117.52 | 6.8 | 8.0 |
| 4 | 2.32 | 126.80 | 7.9 | 8.6 |
| 5 | 2.95½ | 138.62 | 9.3 | 9.3 |

**40th Issue**
**Sold at £25 a unit from 7 December 1992 – 16 December 1993**
**(40th Reinvestment Issue from 13 November 1992)**
*Compound interest rate over first five years = 5.75%*

| Year | Interest: 3 monthly £ | Value anniversary of purchase £ | Yield anniversary of purchase % | Average yield to end term % |
|---|---|---|---|---|
| 1 | 1.00* | 26.00 | 4.0 | 5.8 |
| 2 | 0.28½ | 27.14 | 4.4 | 6.2 |
| 3 | 0.39 | 29.70 | 5.8 | 6.8 |
| 4 | 0.48½ | 30.64 | 6.8 | 7.3 |
| 5 | 0.60½ | 33.06 | 7.9 | 7.9 |

**41st Issue**
**Sold at £25 a unit from 17 December 1993**
*Compound interest rate over first five years = 5.4%*

| Year | Interest: 3 monthly £ | Value anniversary of purchase £ | Yield anniversary of purchase % | Average yield to end term % |
|---|---|---|---|---|
| 1 | 0.9125* | 25.91 | 3.65 | 5.40 |
| 2 | 0.2624 | 26.96 | 4.05 | 5.84 |
| 3 | 0.3640 | 28.42 | 5.40 | 6.44 |
| 4 | 0.4547 | 30.24 | 6.40 | 6.97 |
| 5 | 0.5707 | 32.52 | 7.55 | 7.55 |

37th–41st Issues
* Paid at end of first twelve months.

**Capital Bond Series "A"**
**Sold at £100 a unit from 4 January 1989 – 16 June 1990**
*Gross compound interest rate over first five years = 12%*

| Year | Annual gross interest £ | Value anniversary of purchase £ | Gross yield anniversary of purchase % | Net[1] yield anniversary of purchase % | Gross average yield to end term % | Net[1] average yield to end term % |
|---|---|---|---|---|---|---|
| 4 | 18.51 | 146.14 | 14.5 | 10.9 | 17.6 | 13.2 |
| 5 | 30.10 | 176.24 | 20.6 | 15.5 | 20.6 | 15.5 |

**Capital Bond Series "B"**
**Sold at £100 a unit from 24 June 1990–14 March 1991**
*Gross compound interest rate over first five years = 13%*

| Year | Annual gross interest | Value anniversary of purchase | Gross yield anniversary of purchase | Net[1] yield anniversary of purchase | Gross yield anniversary of purchase | Net[1] yield anniversary of purchase |
|---|---|---|---|---|---|---|
| | £ | £ | % | % | % | % |
| 3 | 14.95 | 134.57 | 12.5 | 9.4 | 15.5 | 11.6 |
| 4 | 20.52 | 155.09 | 15.25 | 11.4 | 17.0 | 12.7 |
| 5 | 29.16 | 184.25 | 18.8 | 14.1 | 18.8 | 14.1 |

**Capital Bond Series "C"**
**Sold at £100 a unit from 2 April 1991–2 May 1992**
*Gross compound interest rate over five years = 11.5%*

| Year | Annual gross interest | Value anniversary of purchase | Gross yield anniversary of purchase | Net[1] yield anniversary of purchase | Gross average yield to end term | Net[1] average yield to end term |
|---|---|---|---|---|---|---|
| | £ | £ | % | % | % | % |
| 2 | 9.36 | 116.36 | 8.8 | 6.6 | 12.7 | 9.5 |
| 3 | 12.80 | 129.16 | 11.0 | 8.3 | 14.0 | 10.5 |
| 4 | 17.76 | 146.92 | 13.8 | 10.3 | 15.5 | 11.6 |
| 5 | 25.42 | 172.34 | 17.3 | 13.0 | 17.3 | 13.0 |

**Capital Bond Series "D"**
**Sold at £100 a unit from 13 May 1992–5 August 1992**
*Gross compound interest rate over first five years = 10.75%*

| Year | Annual gross interest | Value anniversary of purchase | Gross yield anniversary of purchase | Net[1] yield anniversary of purchase | Gross average yield to end term | Net[1] average yield to end term |
|---|---|---|---|---|---|---|
| | £ | £ | % | % | % | % |
| 2 | 8.79 | 115.99 | 8.2 | 6.2 | 11.7 | 8.1 |
| 3 | 11.25 | 127.24 | 9.7 | 7.3 | 12.8 | 8.7 |
| 4 | 15.44 | 142.68 | 12.1 | 9.1 | 14.4 | 9.6 |
| 5 | 23.94 | 166.62 | 16.8 | 12.5 | 16.7 | 10.6 |

**Capital Bond Series "E"**
**Sold at £100 a unit from 24 August 1992 – 22 September 1992**
*Gross compound interest rate over five years = 10%*

| Year | Annual gross interest | Value anniversary of purchase | Gross yield anniversary of purchase | Net[1] yield anniversary of purchase | Gross average yield to end term | Net[1] average yield to end term |
|---|---|---|---|---|---|---|
| | £ | £ | % | % | % | % |
| 2 | 8.6 | 115.56 | 8.0 | 6.0 | 10.7 | 8.0 |
| 3 | 10.98 | 126.54 | 9.5 | 7.1 | 11.7 | 8.7 |
| 4 | 14.55 | 141.09 | 11.5 | 8.6 | 12.8 | 9.6 |
| 5 | 19.96 | 161.05 | 14.2 | 10.6 | 14.1 | 10.6 |

**Capital Bond Series "F"**
**Sold at £100 a unit from 5 October 1992 – 12 November 1992**
*Gross compound interest rate over five years = 9%*

| Year | Annual gross interest | Value anniversary of purchase | Gross yield anniversary of purchase | Net[1] yield anniversary of purchase | Gross average yield to end term | Net[1] average yield to end term |
|---|---|---|---|---|---|---|
| | £ | £ | % | % | % | % |
| 2 | 7.43 | 113.53 | 7.0 | 5.3 | 9.7 | 7.3 |
| 3 | 10.22 | 123.75 | 9.0 | 6.8 | 10.6 | 8.0 |
| 4 | 12.99 | 136.74 | 10.5 | 7.9 | 11.5 | 8.6 |
| 5 | 17.16 | 153.90 | 12.6 | 9.4 | 12.6 | 9.4 |

**Capital Bond Series "G"**
**Sold at £100 a unit from 7 December 1992 – 16 December 1993**
*Gross compound interest rate over five years = 7.75%*

| Year | Annual gross interest | Value anniversary of purchase | Gross yield anniversary of purchase | Net[1] yield anniversary of purchase | Gross average yield to end term | Net[1] average yield to end term |
|---|---|---|---|---|---|---|
| | £ | £ | % | % | % | % |
| 1 | 5.30 | 105.30 | 5.3 | 4.0 | 7.8 | 5.8 |
| 2 | 6.21 | 111.51 | 5.9 | 4.4 | 8.3 | 6.3 |
| 3 | 8.59 | 120.10 | 7.7 | 5.8 | 9.2 | 6.9 |
| 4 | 10.80 | 130.90 | 9.0 | 6.8 | 9.9 | 7.5 |
| 5 | 14.33 | 145.23 | 11.0 | 8.2 | 11.0 | 8.2 |

**Capital Bond Series "H"**
**Sold at £100 a unit from 17 December 1993**
*Gross compound interest rate over five years = 7%*

| Year | Annual gross interest £ | Value anniversary of purchase £ | Gross yield anniversary of purchase % | Net[1] yield anniversary of purchase % | Gross average yield to end term % | Net[1] average yield to end term % |
|---|---|---|---|---|---|---|
| 1 | 4.90 | 104.90 | 4.9 | 3.68 | 7.25 | 5.44 |
| 2 | 5.72 | 110.62 | 5.45 | 4.09 | 7.84 | 5.88 |
| 3 | 8.07 | 118.69 | 7.30 | 5.48 | 8.66 | 6.49 |
| 4 | 9.97 | 128.66 | 8.40 | 6.30 | 9.34 | 7.01 |
| 5 | 13.24 | 141.90 | 10.29 | 7.72 | 10.29 | 7.72 |

**Children's Bonus Bond**
**Sold at £25 a unit**

| Issue on sale | Interest p.a. 1st four years % | Bonus 5th anniversary % | Return to 5th anniversary % | Value 5th anniversary £ |
|---|---|---|---|---|
| Issue "A" 8/7/91 – 2/5/92 | 5.0 | 47.36 | 11.84 | 43.75 |
| Issue "B" 23/5/92 – 5/8/92 | 5.0 | 40.12 | 10.90 | 41.94 |
| Issue "C" 24/8/92 – 22/9/92 | 5.0 | 34.16 | 10.10 | 40.45 |
| Issue "D" 5/10/92 – 12/11/92 | 5.0 | 26.96 | 9.10 | 38.65 |
| Issue "E" 7/12/92 – 16/12/93 | 5.0 | 18.28 | 7.85 | 36.48 |
| Issue "F" 17/12/93 | 5.0 | 14.92 | 7.35 | |

**FIRST Option Bond**
**Sold at £1,000 minimum**

| Purchase date | Guaranteed rate first 12 months** gross % | Guaranteed rate first 12 months** net % | Bonus on £20,000 plus gross % | Bonus on £20,000 plus net % |
|---|---|---|---|---|
| 7/7/92 – 21/7/92 (12 noon) | 10.34 | 7.75 | 0.4 | 0.3 |
| 21/7/92 – 4/10/92 (12 noon) | 9.67 | 7.25 | 0.4 | 0.3 |
| 5/10/92 – 12/11/92 | 8.67 | 6.50 | 0.4 | 0.3 |
| 22/3/93 – 16/12/93 | 6.34 | 4.75 | 0.4 | 0.3 |
| 17/12/93 | 6.00 | 4.50 | 0.4 | 0.3 |

Capital Bond Series "A"–"H"
Interest is added at the end of each twelve months.
[1] Net of basic rate tax at 25%.
** FIRST Option Bond: anniversary interest for the next twelve months at the current guaranteed rate.

# General Extension Rates: Interest Variable

After the fixed term ends, interest, at the GER, is added every three months, although interest is calculated monthly at the rate in force at the beginning of each month.

17 June 1982 to 30 November 1982 8.4%
1 December 1982 to 31 August 1983 7.08%
1 September 1983 to 31 March 1984 7.68%
1 April 1984 to 31 July 1984 6.84%
1 August 1984 to 30 November 1984 8.52%
1 December 1984 to 31 January 1985 8.28%
1 February 1985 to 31 March 1985 9%
1 April 1985 to 30 September 1985 9.51%
1 October 1985 to 31 October 1986 8.01%
1 November 1986 to 31 March 1987 8.7%
1 April 1987 to 31 April 1987 7.5%
1 May 1987 to 30 September 1987 7.02%
1 October 1987 to 29 February 1988 6.51%
1 March 1988 to 30 April 1988 5.76%
1 May 1988 to 30 November 1992 5.01%
1 December 1992 to 31 December 1993 3.75%
1 January 1994 3.51%

The current rate can be obtained at your local post office, by phoning 071–605 9461 or looking on Prestel page 5004213. The following Ansaphone numbers will also provide the current rate:
South – London – 071–605 9483/9484
North – Lytham St Anne's – 0253 723714
Scotland – Glasgow – 041–632 2766

# Older Issues of National Savings Certificates

**1st to 6th Issues**
**Sold between February 1916 and November 1939**

Sell immediately. They yield between 1.2% and 2% a year.

**Decimal, 7th, 8th, 9th, 10th, 11th, 12th, 14th, 16th, 18th, 19th, 21st, 23rd, 24th, 25th, 26th, 27th, 28th, 29th, 30th, 31st, 32nd and 33rd**
All units now earn variable General Extension Rate interest every 3 months; currently 3.51%

There are no 13th, 15th, 17th, 20th and 22nd Issues

# Appendix 3

## The Retail Prices Index

The Retail Prices Index is the official measure of inflation or the cost of living. On the second Tuesday of each month about 300–400 employees from benefit offices around the country check the prices of over 600 goods and services purchased by typical families. These are collated by the Department of Employment and issued as an index number released on the second or third Friday of the following month. The index was re-based in January 1987 to take account of changes in our shopping habits, so all subsequent index numbers will appear lower than those listed on page **172**, which have not been adjusted for the change.

## Index-Linked Savings Certificates

When you buy National Savings Index-Linked Certificates the index number which is used to work out the subsequent rise in the value of your certificates is the one for two months earlier. If you buy certificates in June, it is the April index number – which is published in May – which is the starting base.

When you encash your certificate, the same rules apply. The cash-in value of your certificates in June will relate to the April index-linked value, published in May.

On the Wednesday following publication of the RPI, *Money Mail* gives the latest value of certificates if they are sold the *next* month. As eight working days' notice is required, the following month is the earliest date at which the certificates can be encashed.

**UK Retail Prices Index – 1920 to 1992**

| | 1920 | 1921 | 1922 | 1923 | 1924 | 1925 |
|---|---|---|---|---|---|---|
| **Average** | 27.7 | 25.1 | 20.4 | 19.4 | 19.5 | 19.6 |
| | **1926** | **1927** | **1928** | **1929** | **1930** | **1931** |
| **Average** | 19.1 | 18.7 | 18.5 | 18.2 | 17.6 | 16.4 |
| | **1932** | **1933** | **1934** | **1935** | **1936** | **1937** |
| **Average** | 16.0 | 15.6 | 15.7 | 15.9 | 16.4 | 17.2 |
| | **1938** | **1939–45** | **1946** | **1947** | **1948** | **1949** |
| **Average** | 17.4 | na | 29.4 | 31.4 | 33.8 | 34.6 |
| | **1950** | **1951** | **1952** | **1953** | **1954** | **1955** |
| **Average** | 35.6 | 38.8 | 41.2 | 41.9 | 42.6 | 44.1 |
| | **1956** | **1957** | **1958** | **1959** | **1960** | **1961** |
| **Average** | 46.0 | 47.5 | 48.8 | 49.1 | 49.6 | 51.0 |
| | **1962** | **1963** | **1964** | **1965** | **1966** | **1967** |
| **Average** | 53.0 | 54.0 | 55.8 | 58.4 | 60.7 | 62.3 |
| | **1968** | **1969** | **1970** | **1971** | **1972** | **1973** |
| **Average** | 65.2 | 68.7 | 73.1 | 80.0 | 85.7 | 93.5 |
| | **1974** | **1975** | **1976** | **1977** | **1978** | **1979** |
| **Average** | 108.5 | 134.8 | 157.1 | 182.0 | 197.1 | 223.5 |
| **Jan** | 100.0 | 119.9 | 147.9 | 172.4 | 189.5 | 207.2 |
| **Feb** | 101.7 | 121.9 | 149.8 | 174.1 | 190.6 | 208.9 |
| **March** | 102.6 | 124.3 | 150.6 | 175.8 | 191.8 | 210.6 |
| **April** | 106.1 | 129.1 | 153.5 | 180.3 | 194.6 | 214.2 |
| **May** | 107.6 | 134.5 | 155.2 | 181.7 | 195.7 | 215.9 |
| **June** | 108.7 | 137.1 | 156.0 | 183.6 | 197.2 | 219.6 |
| **July** | 109.7 | 138.5 | 156.3 | 183.8 | 198.1 | 229.1 |
| **Aug** | 109.8 | 139.3 | 158.5 | 184.7 | 199.4 | 230.9 |
| **Sept** | 111.0 | 140.5 | 160.6 | 185.7 | 200.2 | 233.2 |
| **Oct** | 113.2 | 142.5 | 163.5 | 186.5 | 201.1 | 235.6 |
| **Nov** | 115.2 | 144.2 | 165.8 | 187.4 | 202.5 | 237.7 |
| **Dec** | 116.9 | 146.0 | 168.0 | 188.4 | 204.2 | 239.4 |

| | 1980 | 1981 | 1982 | 1983 | 1984 | 1985 | 1986 | 1987 |
|---|---|---|---|---|---|---|---|---|
| **Average** | 263.7 | 295.0 | 320.4 | 335.1 | 351.7 | 373.2 | 385.9 | 101.9 |
| **Jan** | 245.3 | 277.3 | 310.6 | 325.9 | 342.6 | 359.8 | 379.7 | 100.0 |
| **Feb** | 248.8 | 279.8 | 310.7 | 327.3 | 344.0 | 362.7 | 381.1 | 100.4 |
| **March** | 252.2 | 284.0 | 313.4 | 327.9 | 345.1 | 366.1 | 381.6 | 100.6 |
| **April** | 260.8 | 292.2 | 319.7 | 332.5 | 349.7 | 373.9 | 385.3 | 101.8 |
| **May** | 263.2 | 294.1 | 322.0 | 333.9 | 351.0 | 375.6 | 386.0 | 101.9 |
| **June** | 265.7 | 295.8 | 322.9 | 334.7 | 351.9 | 376.4 | 385.8 | 101.9 |
| **July** | 267.9 | 297.1 | 323.0 | 336.5 | 351.5 | 375.7 | 384.7 | 101.8 |
| **Aug** | 268.5 | 299.3 | 323.1 | 338.0 | 354.8 | 376.7 | 385.9 | 102.1 |
| **Sept** | 270.2 | 301.0 | 322.9 | 339.5 | 355.5 | 376.5 | 387.8 | 102.4 |
| **Oct** | 271.9 | 303.7 | 324.5 | 340.7 | 357.7 | 377.1 | 388.4 | 102.9 |
| **Nov** | 274.1 | 306.9 | 326.1 | 341.9 | 358.8 | 378.4 | 391.7 | 103.4 |
| **Dec** | 275.6 | 308.8 | 325.5 | 342.8 | 358.5 | 378.9 | 393.0 | 103.3 |

| | 1988 | 1989 | 1990 | 1991 | 1992 | 1993 |
|---|---|---|---|---|---|---|
| **Average** | 106.3 | 115.2 | 126.1 | 133.5 | 138.5 | 140.7 |
| **Jan** | 103.3 | 111.0 | 119.5 | 130.2 | 135.6 | 137.9 |
| **Feb** | 103.3 | 111.8 | 120.2 | 130.9 | 136.3 | 138.8 |
| **March** | 103.7 | 112.3 | 121.4 | 131.4 | 136.7 | 139.3 |
| **April** | 104.1 | 114.3 | 125.1 | 133.1 | 138.8 | 140.6 |
| **May** | 105.8 | 115.0 | 126.2 | 133.5 | 139.3 | 141.1 |
| **June** | 106.2 | 115.4 | 126.7 | 134.1 | 139.3 | 141.0 |
| **July** | 106.6 | 115.5 | 126.8 | 133.8 | 138.8 | 140.7 |
| **Aug** | 106.7 | 115.8 | 128.1 | 134.1 | 138.9 | 141.3 |
| **Sept** | 107.9 | 116.6 | 129.3 | 134.6 | 139.4 | 141.9 |
| **Oct** | 108.4 | 117.5 | 130.3 | 135.1 | 139.9 | 141.8 |
| **Nov** | 109.5 | 118.5 | 130.0 | 135.6 | 139.7 | 141.6 |
| **Dec** | 110.0 | 118.8 | 129.9 | 135.7 | 139.2 | 141.9 |

Index rebased January 1987 = 100. Divide "old" index numbers by 3.945 to convert to new base.

Source: Central Statistics Office. For later numbers phone 071–270 6363/6364

# Appendix 4

## CAR: The Real Rate of Interest

The flat investment interest rates quoted by banks and building societies are sometimes followed by a slightly higher rate and the letters CAR. This stands for "compound annual rate".

If you reinvest your income in the same account, rather than spend it, it can affect the real rate of interest you receive. Interest paid more frequently than once a year and reinvested itself begins to earn interest. And interest on interest adds up to a slightly higher interest rate than the flat quoted rate.

The compound effect of interest paid at intervals ranging from monthly to annually can add up to useful extra interest on larger investments, particularly when interest rates in general are high. If you spend your income, only the flat rate is relevant.

**Compounded Annual Interest Rates**

| Quoted rate* % | Compounded annual rate when interest is Annually % | Half-yearly % | Quarterly % | Monthly % |
|---|---|---|---|---|
| 5.00 | 5.00 | 5.06 | 5.09 | 5.12 |
| 5.50 | 5.50 | 5.58 | 5.61 | 5.64 |
| 6.00 | 6.00 | 6.09 | 6.14 | 6.17 |
| 6.50 | 6.50 | 6.61 | 6.66 | 6.70 |
| 7.00 | 7.00 | 7.12 | 7.19 | 7.23 |
| 7.50 | 7.50 | 7.64 | 7.71 | 7.76 |
| 8.00 | 8.00 | 8.16 | 8.24 | 8.30 |
| 8.50 | 8.50 | 8.68 | 8.77 | 8.84 |
| 9.00 | 9.00 | 9.20 | 9.31 | 9.38 |
| 9.50 | 9.50 | 9.73 | 9.84 | 9.92 |
| 10.00 | 10.00 | 10.25 | 10.38 | 10.47 |
| 10.50 | 10.50 | 10.78 | 10.92 | 11.02 |
| 11.00 | 11.00 | 11.30 | 11.46 | 11.57 |
| 11.50 | 11.50 | 11.83 | 12.01 | 12.13 |
| 12.00 | 12.00 | 12.36 | 12.55 | 12.68 |
| 12.50 | 12.50 | 12.89 | 13.10 | 13.24 |
| 13.00 | 13.00 | 13.42 | 13.65 | 13.80 |
| 13.50 | 13.50 | 13.96 | 14.20 | 14.37 |
| 14.00 | 14.00 | 14.49 | 14.75 | 14.93 |
| 14.50 | 14.50 | 15.03 | 15.31 | 15.50 |
| 15.00 | 15.00 | 15.56 | 15.87 | 16.08 |

* Net rate. Interest is taxable even if it is reinvested, so taxpayers cannot benefit in full from the compound gross interest.

# Appendix 5

## National Savings Pensioners Guaranteed Income Bonds

A lump sum investment, dubbed the 'Granny Bond' paying monthly interest without deduction of tax at source. Interest is fixed for five years.

| | |
|---|---|
| Suitable for | Retired people who want a fixed level of monthly income and do not need access to their capital. |
| Open to | Those aged 65 and over only. |
| Min–Max | £500/£20,000. |
| Charges | None. |
| Withdrawals | 60 days notice and no interest is paid during the notice period if you want your money back before the end of five years. |
| Interest | Fixed at 7 per cent for five year, paid monthly. |
| Tax | Not deducted, but interest is taxable so should be declared on your tax form. |
| How to invest | Application forms available at post offices or by post from National Savings, Blackpool FY3 9YP, or by telephone 0500 500 000. |
| Money Mail | ***** |

# Index